Pride:

The Story of the First Openly Gay Navy SEAL

D1260815

by
Brett Jones

First published by Dog Ear Publishing
4010 W. 86th Street, Ste H
Indianapolis, IN 46268
www.dogearpublishing.net

ISBN: 978-1-4575-3107-1

Library of Congress Control Number: has been applied for

This book is printed on acid-free paper.

Some names have been changed in this book to protect the privacy of the individuals involved.

Printed in the United States of America

Dedicated to:

Jason Allen White

"*I got nothing that I asked for, but everything I hoped for. Almost despite myself, my unspoken prayers were answered. I am, among all men, most richly blessed.*"

—Unknown Confederate Soldier

Dedicated to:

Jason Allen White

"I got nothing that I asked for, but everything I hoped for. Almost despite myself, my unspoken prayers were answered. I am, among all men, most richly blessed."

—Unknown Confederate Soldier

Foreword

It has been my experience that most of the men I've worked with in the Special Operations community are more concerned with an individual's contribution to the team, and their ability to do their job exceptionally well, than their race or sexual preferences. It's meritocracy in its purest form, and an excellent example set by the people who make up the Special Operations Operations. However, as I write this, transgendered men and women cannot openly serve in the US military, they are forced to hide their true identities in order to serve their country, and this needs to change. As you read on you'll come to know that Brett Jones is all too familiar with this dilemma.

Jones's story is proof that gays in Special Operations roles existed long before the inception and eventual death of Don't-Ask-Don't-Tell (DADT). And while politicians and religious fanatics made a fuss about gays serving in the military, these men and women proudly served their country in solitude, and went on to earn the respect of their peers.

Brett's story isn't about being a gay SEAL; it's about a human being overcoming incredible odds and adversity to pursue his hopes and dreams. The lessons and stories you will come to know in his book can be applied to people from all walks of life. I was a Basic Underwater Demolition/SEAL Training (BUD/S) 215 classmate of Brett's, and had no idea he was gay, while together, we went through one of the toughest training courses the US military has to offer. Brett Jones earned the US Navy SEAL Trident, I am proud to have served with him, endorse his story, and to call him my friend.

—Brandon Webb, Former Navy SEAL & Editor of Sofrep.com

In Danger

I hung up the payphone with my head hanging towards the ground. "Fuck. Fuck. Fuck! How could they possibly have found out that I am gay? I am always so careful. I am always really careful. Somebody must have informed on me... but who? Who do I know that would do such a thing? Take a breath, Brett, and just breathe. Just. Breathe. Dammit," I thought to myself while exhaling deeply. I looked over to the gate and saw that my flight had already started boarding.

The line moved fairly quickly. "Have a nice flight, Mr. Jones," the airline representative said with a simulated smile. I nodded and made my way past the scanner onto the jet bridge. I felt like a lamb being herded to the slaughterhouse, a lamb of an unattractive color, an individual amongst the flock. I had blended in so well for so long. It turned my stomach to realize I'd been marked for the appetites of others.

Of course I was in a middle seat. Why would it be anything else? "Fuck it," I thought, "I really don't care. Even if I were in first class, it would not change how I feel or what is about to happen."

The guy sitting in the aisle seat would not even get up. He just kept staring forward as he pulled in his legs. I sighed, rolled my eyes, and squished my way into the seat, not caring how much of my ass was in his face. Using what little room I had to find the female end of the seatbelt, I took a deep breath, tried to relax, and clicked the buckle together. I hoped the clicking noise would somehow end the anxiety.

The flight attendants did their thing, but only served as background noise; I was someplace else altogether. Today I was a Navy SEAL. In fact, just the night before I had jumped out of a plane in Yuma, Arizona, at twenty thousand feet, on oxygen, with a full combat load.

So many years of hard work... so much was about to be taken from me.

Turning my head, I looked across the man sitting next to me and gazed out his window as we taxied on the tarmac.

The airplane got comfortably loud as the engines roared and we hurtled down the runway. As the plane slowly left the ground, I felt the force of gravity gently pulling me back into my seat.

Staring out the oval window I thought to myself, "I really hate flying." Almost every SEAL I'd ever worked with had had some sort of bad helicopter or fixed-wing aircraft accident, including myself.

I will never forget that clear night on the flight deck of our aircraft carrier, the USS Dwight D. Eisenhower.

We were cruising somewhere off the coast of North Carolina. The United States was at war with itself. Well, not officially. But every so often they would have the same readiness exercise to prepare the US Armed Forces, including the special warfare community, for war.

The plan was to split our platoon into two eight-man fire teams. We would separate onto the two Blackhawks on the deck of the carrier. They would fly us about two kilometers away from a makeshift village that had been built on a shooting range for our training. We would make our way to the target and set up for a raid. The left flank would hose down the target with a tremendous amount of firepower. Afterwards, the other flank would move in to collect intelligence, set charges, and blow up a radio tower. We would then quickly head back to the extraction point.

We made our way across the flight deck through a flurry of powerful wind and loaded up into the blacked-out and gutted Blackhawks. This was not unusual; fitting eight fully-loaded guys into a small Blackhawk required all the seats to be removed. We lifted off the ground and started flying west towards the mainland.

As we got closer to land, the birds flew up to ten thousand feet to avoid any simulated surface-to-air missiles. The helicopter descended towards the infiltration point and I used my hands to feel my gear in the dark. I often did this to give myself a last minute warm and fuzzy on the readiness of all my weapon systems.

Being a 60 gunner was awesome. I carried the most firepower on the team. The only part that sucked was humping the 21 pound fully automatic M60 machine gun plus 500–700 rounds (weighing roughly 35–50 pounds) to the target, in addition to all my other gear and water.

As soon as we arrived on target we got the signal from the other mobile flank. Lying flat on the ground behind a small berm on the edge of a tree line I looked through my sights, turned off the safety, and let that gun do its job on the target. My unspoken goal was to burn through as much of that ammo as possible. The more I shot, the less I had to carry home. My ammo changes were perfect. There was hardly a lull between them. When I got the ceasefire to allow the other team to move in I had only two hundred rounds left. The barrel of the machine gun was glowing a bright red-orange and the wooden building looked like Swiss cheese. The actions on the target went flawlessly.

We made our way back to the extraction point, called the pilots, and quickly loaded up for the flight back to the ship.

Flying back was just a reverse of the route in. We flew up to ten thousand feet and headed back out to sea. Fifteen minutes into the flight, the helicopter started vibrating and shuddering. Moments later we heard a loud thumping above, followed by the unmistakable sound of an object being thrown very fast away from us. It sounded as if a piece of the chopper had broken off and was flung violently away.

The lights in the cockpit started going crazy.

The crew chief was manning the door gun, while the rest of us were piled in the belly of the bird. He looked frantic. Obviously talking with the pilots over his headset, he let go of his push-to-talk button, turned to us, and said, "Everyone hold on to each other! We are going down!"

There was no door on the opposite side of the helicopter adjacent to the crew chief. Being only one foot away from the open door, I immediately grabbed ahold of the two guys sitting closest to me. As we dropped, the helicopter stayed relatively upright. Looking around, I saw no evidence of land.

"We are going to hit the water," I mumbled to myself. Immediately, I went back to my helicopter dunker training. We had all been through it at some point to prepare us to escape a sinking helicopter.

Falling from ten thousand feet takes a long time. It gave me a lot of time to think. "Forgive me, God, for anything I have ever done against your will."

At that moment I felt a warm composure move over me from His presence.

"I know you're with me. I can feel you. I can feel you. I can feel you. I know you're with me."

The helicopter started shaking violently as it fell. "Let's get this over with." I prayed, having no expectation of surviving this crash.

What seemed like an eternity later, the helicopter auto-rotated, which allowed the air rushing up from the ground to spin the blades and create just enough lift to land safely.

The lack of light caused me to think that we were still over water, but we were actually still over land. The pilots miraculously landed the helicopter; it was a rough landing, but a landing nonetheless. The pilots bailed out immediately. Still in shock that we were all somehow still alive, we followed their lead and rallied a few hundred feet away to get a head count. Everyone was alive.

I looked over at one of the older guys who had mentored me over the past year. On his hand was written the name of his wife and daughter. He had used the grease pen attached to his gear to write their names as we fell to the earth. It was his intention to let them know that they were that last people he'd thought about in this life.

"It's time for a fucking drink! What do you say, Jonesy?" he said, laughing as he saw that I'd caught him staring at his hand.

"Oh yeah!" I replied with a deep exhale, turning my gaze towards the downed chopper.

Back in the present, as my plane started its twenty-minute descent into Norfolk I fought back a single, stubborn tear for that night and how much those guys meant to me. I felt a comforting numbness slowly creep in—a self-defense mechanism I had developed years ago to protect myself from humiliation and shame. I reached up and opened the air conditioning nozzle and pointed it toward my face. The plane soon landed and made its way to the gate.

I floated off the plane, and glided down the long airport terminal, completely oblivious to anyone or anything around me. As I got closer to the escalator going down, I could see the unmistakable camouflage uniform of the SEAL team command master chief, waiting for me by the baggage claim.

As I approached him, I started to blur my eyes—another self-defense mechanism that allowed me to stare somebody directly in the eyes, without actually looking them in the eyes, thus keeping me from becoming emotional.

"I am going to get the car and pull it around front. Meet me out there when you get your luggage," he said.

"Okay. No problem, master chief," I responded confidently. We turned away from each other. In that moment, a tear found its opportunity and crested itself in the corner of my right eye. Quickly and casually I wiped it away without anyone noticing, took in a deep breath through my nose, and focused on finding my luggage.

CHAPTER 1

Purgatorium

The world is an evil place. The world is a beautiful place. The world is complex and simple. It shifts and moves, slowly changing those in it. It connects us, and it drives us apart. It can show us great kindness, and it can cruelly take from us.

I don't pretend to understand how the world works as a whole. Instead of focusing on the big picture, I try to focus on what actually makes sense to me. As human beings, we try to put things in perspective by identifying ourselves in others. We can look at an old homeless man on the side of the road and in a millisecond determine that person is a lazy drunk. There is a good probability that, minus some important details, we are right. However, we can empathize with him because we know what it is like to be lazy; and all of us on some level know what an addiction feels like and that we are all just a few bad choices away from holding up a sign on a street corner.

We are all at some point along an emotional spectrum. We have done horrible things and wonderful things in our lives, thus giving us the power to identify with each other.

My name is Brett Jones, and I was born in 1974. My name has meant different things to different people over my lifetime, and I imagine that it will likely continue to do so. I know that the only thing that I will take to my grave is my name. Unlike most people in the world, I have two names. I was born with the first, and the second I received later in life. Both are very important to me, and both have equal accountability.

As a child, I struggled with Attention Deficit Hyperactivity Disorder (ADHD), borderline personality disorder, and was extremely hyperactive. In short, I was a little monster. I threw chairs at teachers, stabbed babysitters, whipped my brother with a chain. I hit my own mother. To say that I am embarrassed only begins to touch on the matter. Thank God I somehow got through it without killing anybody or ending up in jail.

My father is a decorated Vietnam fighter pilot, and my mother is the daughter of a World War II fighter pilot. They had three children, about two years apart each—Marc, the oldest, Tracey, the youngest, and me.

My mother would tell me later in life that she knew there was something wrong with me at a very early age. She would do her best to comfort me as a crying baby, but there were times when none of the normal motherly things would work. She said I would scream uncontrollably, and then shake violently in the crib with what she described as rage.

My earliest memory was when I was two years old. We were living in Ramstein, Germany, and I somehow managed to find my way out of our apartment. I crawled to the stairwell just outside the door. I remember crawling to the edge and looking down the two stories to the bottom.

I can't remember much after that, but my father would later recount how he felt when he saw me with a broken back in the hospital. He said, "I knew something really bad had happened to you because you did not cry. You just laid there and silently moaned."

I had no regard for my own welfare. In fact, I was so accident-prone as a child that my parents were terrified that they were just one emergency room visit away from being investigated by child welfare. I can't begin to imagine the trouble that I put them through. I believe that raising a child with ADHD is no easy task, even for the most saintly of people.

My mother became a born-again Christian when I was very young. She was very insistent that all of us be raised that way. Additionally, she became a health food fanatic. She found it was the only way to somewhat moderate my behavior. Sugar became an outlawed substance in our house.

Even then, I was very well aware that I was a bad kid. Looking back at those days, I have no idea what would have helped me. My parents tried everything from drugs, shrinks, pastors... even a good old fashioned exorcism. Yeah, that's right. Apparently by pinning your son's shoulders against the wall and yelling these words, "I command you, demon, to get out of my son... I rebuke you in the name of Jesus!" you can get him to stop acting crazy. It worked several times.

I can't say that I blame her. Here is this woman who was basically left to raise three kids on her own.

My father was a career-minded Air Force officer who spent a lot of his time away from home. He is an extremely intelligent man. However, he was absent from many important events in our family. Whenever he found himself in a situation with the family, it was apparent that he was very uncomfortable. It would be easy to say that this was because the amount of alcohol that he drank on a daily basis. Drinking disconnected him so much from our family, but I don't think that is necessarily the problem. There is usually a reason a person drinks that way. For years I wondered if it was my bad behavior, or if it had something to do with Vietnam. Truth is, only he really knows why he bailed emotionally on being a father.

I feel that I should make it clear that I do love my father, but not as a child would normally love a father. Perhaps it is closer to how one would love an uncle. We can't choose our parents, and looking back I am very thankful for the ones I have. Still, I grew up daydreaming of having a different dad. I would be so jealous of my friends and the relationship they had with their fathers. Alone in my room I found myself often daydreaming that Indiana Jones was my real dad, and that one day very soon he would come and rescue me.

On one particularly hot summer afternoon when I was about five, a person entered our house. I was on my belly lying on the floor by the living room couch. The person quickly straddled me, turned me over, pinned my arms under their knees, and placed a pillow over my face so fast that I never saw who it was.

I remember struggling at first because I could barely breathe. Quickly turning my head to the side, I was able to get a quick lung full of air and a momentary glimpse of the couch before my attacker forced my face back under the pillow. It was a very plain couch. The carpet was a dull brown and the walls and floorboards under the couch were white. The only real color I saw was the navy blue fabric of the pillow as my face was forced back into position. I very consciously thought to myself, "Act like you're dead, and it will stop." I am not sure how long I remained still under the pressure of that pillow, but it seemed like an eternity.

A strange thing happened during those moments. Though my body was cringing for air and I felt myself losing consciousness, I was somehow able to relax and accept that I was going to die.

Moments later, I was released. I dared not move. The pillow was left covering my face and the person departed very quickly.

This became a pivotal point in my life. I remember wishing the person had just kept that pillow over me a little bit longer. If only that individual had fully committed, I could be

with Jesus and not living with the guilt of constantly upsetting the people I loved.

I never spoke of this incident to anyone. I felt like I deserved it, and honestly did not want to know, or was afraid to find out who it might have been.

People have told me that at such a young age no one has a real concept of mortality. Nothing could be further from the truth in my case. I knew exactly what dying was, probably better than I can comprehend now, and I had absolutely no problems with or fear of it. I just did not want it to be painful. I thought of all of the stories that my mother had told me about Jesus and how fun heaven would be. It sounded so much better than constantly hurting my family and making people cry.

It took a couple years for me to stop wishing that every time I hurt myself or other people hurt me that it would somehow kill me. I honestly can't recall a defining moment when I stopped being suicidal; I guess I just slowly grew out of it. However, the allure of dying never left me after that—not because there was a heaven that I would go to, but because there was just nothing that scared me about it. This may be hard for some people to fully understand, but that person who may have or may not have tried to kill me gave me a gift that day.

Being in a Christian family meant trips to church every Sunday, followed by Sunday school. I hated that ritual. In fact the only thing that I liked about Sundays was that we often went to brunch at the officer's club afterwards. They had such a colorful buffet, and it was chock full of my favorite drug— sugar! It almost made the pain of having to sit still through an entire sermon worth it. Almost.

I never had complete faith in what the Bible said. I knew that some of what was being told to me could be true and some of it did contain personal value, but there were just so many holes in it as a whole. Even as a child I could discern that. I actually do believe that faith is important. My problem comes from having been involved with every major world conflict since 1994 and seeing firsthand the results that these religions have on such large numbers of people. The best disguise that hatred has is under the cloak of any given religion.

After being forced to sit through numerous one-on-ones with different pastors and ministers, I eventually learned the only way to make it through these painful meetings was to agree with whatever they said, even if I thought they were full of crap. Inevitably, we would end the meeting with a prayer for God to reveal himself to me, or for Jesus to come into my heart again. Just like clockwork, the pastor would put his hand on my shoulder or knee, as if somehow he could channel Jesus into me. I hated that; it was just plain awkward.

I am often asked what I believe now. I know that there is a God; I know it because I can feel it. I pray to Him, and I have a personal relationship with Him. I don't think any major religion knows the absolute truth or what His will truly is. In fact I think they serve to convolute His will on many disturbing levels.

I have chosen to let my heart guide me,　not a book, and definitely not a person—just as I would in any relationship.

CHAPTER 2

Osan, Korea

In 1980, my family moved to Osan, Korea. It was far from a picture-perfect move. The good ole Air force did a spectacular job getting us there. My father left several days ahead of us, leaving my mother to haul three kids around the world by herself. I imagine it had to be very stressful for her.

I believe our time in Korea was the start of a profound respect that I would always have for my older brother Marc. As a child, he had blonde curly hair, and big teeth (he eventually grew into) with braces that required headgear at night. He loved the Dallas Cowboys, and was never afraid to fight anybody or stand up to bullies. He had the funniest sense of humor, often making people laugh by stating or talking about what was obvious to him; things that seemed to narrowly escape your perception. Something as simple as him talking about buying a Coke out of a vending machine would turn into a comedy act at the dinner table. Marc has always been a very important person in my life. He had the ability to somehow come out of trouble completely unscathed. He was amazing!

My brother and his friends from the fourth grade had discovered a new world just below the surface of our apartment buildings. There was a seemingly endless labyrinth of tunnels and chambers, full of all kinds of mystery.

One of Marc's friends told me a story about these tunnels. There used to be a problem with rats there. The Odishees (Korean groundskeepers) had released a bunch of cats in the tunnel system to eat the rats. It had temporarily solved the problem... until the cats became a huge problem. So they put wild dogs down there to eradicate the cats. Now there are wild dogs living in the dark catacombs underneath these buildings. Holy crap!

One day, my brother allowed me to explore the tunnels with him and his friends, as long as I promised not to tell my mom about it (I had a problem of telling on everybody, even myself, at that age). Before we started, a fifth-grade girl came running to tell Marc how a kid in his class had been caught by the Odishees doing something that he wasn't supposed to do. They were holding him at the housing office at the entrance to the housing area. They hadn't yet figured out who his parents were because none of the groundskeepers spoke English.

Marc immediately jumped into action and came up with a plan. He told the kids that they could use the map that they had already made to find the tunnel system that ran underneath the housing office. They would sneak in and rescue him from indefinite groundation by his parents.

My brother put his plan into action very quickly. We entered the tunnel system from an open grate on the outside of our building, which was in the far back corner of the housing area. I remember staying very close to him as we travelled through what seemed like miles of dark tunnels, moving carefully and quietly enough to avoid waking the dogs (and everybody knows that wild dogs must sleep during the day). Eventually, Marc announced that we had arrived directly underneath the building where his friend was being held.

There was an iron ladder leading up to a hatch. We all climbed up and, sure enough, we were in the housing office. I could not believe that my brother had actually gotten us there. His friend could not believe his eyes either! My brother motioned for the boy to come over to him, and just like that he was free. My brother was a hero! He had single-handedly planned and executed a daring mission against the Odishees!

As it turned out, the kid was in the housing office by himself. The groundskeepers had locked him in to keep him from running away while they attended to maintenance. They had also phoned the base police, who were en route. Luckily for Marc's friend, the Odishees never even got his name.

Marc would later graduate to greater exploits. For example, he would sneak up behind local taxi cab drivers as they were backing up, smack his hands loudly on the trunk, and fall to the ground. The driver would rush out of the car, see him knocked unconscious there, and freak out. Yelling something in Korean, the driver would run to find a phone. That was my brother's cue to quickly leave and join his friends, who had been laughing their asses off at a safe distance.

My brother's dedication to his friends served as an example to me at a young age. It would be years before I fully grasped the true meaning of the word friendship and the great responsibility that came with it.

One day I found myself at the playground in the center of all the buildings. A friend of mine in the second grade was with me, playing in the sand box near a swing set. I remember being bored and asking him, "Do you want to play tag?"

He said in a semi-pouting way, "There are not enough kids to play tag. It's no fun when it's just two kids."

I looked around. There were only two other older kids by the swing set. One of them was a boy named Marcus. He was a black kid in the sixth grade. The rest of us thought he was really cool because he always dressed really well and had about a two-inch afro. The other kid was a younger black girl, maybe in the fifth grade. I looked over at my friend and said, "We could get Marcus to play with us."

He looked up from the sand. Gazing over towards the swing set he said, "He is too old. He will never want to play with second graders."

I stood up from the sand and dusted my pants off, then went over to Marcus and asked, "Hey, do you want to play tag with us?"

He looked down and laughed and said, "Na, I don't want to play." Then he turned away to get back to his conversation with the girl.

I walked back to my friend and said, "He does not want to play."

A few minutes later my friend said, "I know how we could get Marcus to play tag."

I looked up and asked how.

"Go over and ask him if he is a nigger," he replied.

"What is that?" I asked.

"It's a word they used to say… I think in old Bible times, to get black people to chase you."

"I still don't think he is going to want to play," I replied as I stood up and dusted my pants off again. I walked over to Marcus. He was now sitting in one of the swings, with the girl in the swing next to him. As I walked up to him, he stopped his conversation and turned his attention to me.

"Marcus, are you a nigger?" I asked, expecting him to get excited. Instead, his and the girl's faces went from happy and smiling to sad and serious. "Do you want to play tag now?" I asked.

He just stared at me. I could see tears starting to form at the bottom of both his eyes.

Confused, I turned back to my friend in the sand box and I yelled, "What is a nigger?"

My friend got up and started running away. Before I could turn completely around to face Marcus, he had tackled me to the ground, pinned my wrists down next to my head, and was

sitting on my sternum. In shock, I just looked up. His face was not one foot from mine. A tear fell from his eye and landed on my cheek.

He said, "Black people used to be slaves, and that is what they called us."

The girl standing not far away said, "Give that boy a whooping, Marcus!" His eyes never left mine. Still very confused, I just looked up at him. He let go of both my wrists and sat up straight. He looked away for a moment to wipe his face on his sleeve and looked back down at my trembling face and said, "It's a bad word, kid."

He stood up and walked away with the girl.

I immediately went home to tell my brother and my dad what had happened. My dad explained why the word was so offensive. It was so hard for me to comprehend; it made no sense to me that white people would do those things to black people just because they were black. I remember very clearly the seriousness in my dad's face when he told me that I had to go to his apartment and apologize.

My dad got on the phone and called Marcus's dad, while pointing for me to go and apologize. I walked over to the far building where he lived and knocked on the first story door. Marcus opened the door. I could see his father standing in the living room behind him, looking at me. I looked up at Marcus and said, "I am really sorry I called you that..." I started to cry, "That bad word, Marcus" He then stretched his hand out and we shook hands.

His dad walked over to the door and told Marcus to go back and finish his dinner. His dad looked down at me and shook my hand. He then placed his other hand on my shoulder while squatting to my level and said, "You better get back home, son. It's getting dark out."

I walked back to my apartment, still very troubled and confused over the power that one word had over everybody, including my family. What bothered me more specifically was that I was white and would never want to make black people my slave or be mean to them. I didn't understand why black people had become slaves. My brother and my dad had a few more conversations with me to clear up the confusion that remained. My father could not stand racism, and for that I will always be thankful.

The first summer we were in Korea something very interesting happened. There was a pool on the Air Force base that was within walking distance of our apartment building. Just like any other kid I loved going to the pool.

On one particularly hot summer day, a good friend had invited me to go with him and his dad to the pool. We went into the locker room to change first. I had already come prepared with my swim trunks on. I remember watching his dad getting naked. It was all I could do not to stare, but his full-grown body was just so exciting for me to look at.

We entered the pool and started playing, as kids do. I was jumping off of the high dive and trying to convince my friend to follow. After demonstrating how it was done, I swam to the side of the pool to watch him attempt to make the daring plunge. I rested my arm on the side of the pool, and heard the sound of other kids cheering him on. He stood on the edge of the diving board looking at the water two stories below.

A voice from the side was joining in. It was his father. As I turned towards the sound of his voice, I noticed that his dad was laying out on a beach recliner not twenty feet from me. The way he was positioned with his feet facing me, I instantly noticed that I could almost look all the way up his shorts. I scooted down the wall to try and get a better angle when my crotch brushed by a powerful water jet. Something about that felt amazing. I scooted back to the jet and in a matter of seconds a surge of paralyzing energy rushed through my body leaving me out of breath and slightly trembling.

What the hell was that? I remember trying to recreate that feeling many more times on the side of the pool that summer. I laugh now thinking of myself hanging on the edge of the pool. I wonder if anybody had the slightest idea of what I was trying to do. I imagine people thought I was some kind of special child just staring motionless, hanging on the side of the pool.

It was then that I definitively knew that I liked men.

Our family adopted a stray cat while we lived in Korea. I can't remember how we came to own this cat, but my money is on my sister finding it near a dumpster somewhere and bringing it home. Tracey had a very kind heart and the best intentions when it came to animals. She would later graduate to more exotic quarry, from field gophers (which she secretly kept as pets in her bedroom drawer) to much bigger animals like... oh, let's just say a Bengal tiger, two cougars, a parrot, and several dogs, to name a few.

We were all pretty excited about having a new pet cat. The creature was timid at first and did not like to be held. In fact, we learned very quickly not to hold this cat at all because it would claw the hell out of us. We did not think much of it because it was a stray and had probably been abused, had a rough life, or just was not comfortable with its new home. It spent the first night hiding under the living room couch.

The next day all of us kids found some small boxes and brought them back up to the apartment. We built it a really cool three-story house. The bottom floor had just one entrance, and the second and third floors had just one small window each. We cut holes in each of the floors so the cat could easily maneuver between them. The whole house was secured with duct tape and stood three feet high.

Upon completion we went to grab the cat to put him in his new home. It had not moved since we got it. My brother reached under the couch to try and grab it. We heard a low, very deep, grumbling growl. With both his arms already under the couch, my brother turned towards me and my sister with a look of grave concern. For a moment he dared not move.

We stood looking down at him with wide eyes. A loud hiss and ear-piercing screech followed, with my brother violently trying to pull his arms from under the couch. He was able to remove them, revealing about eight long scratches on each of his forearms. He just stood there looking at them. They had already started to bleed. The cat bolted from under the couch to the house we'd made. It shook a couple times, and then it stood silent.

My sister, excited that the cat was in its new house, ran over to get a good look at him. She got on her elbows and knees and peered into the main entrance, making sure to keep about a foot's distance.

The main entrance was fairly small, and not much light could get into it. She rose up off of her elbows and said, "I think he moved to the second floor."

Before my brother could get a word out she had moved in closer. She canted her head to the side to allow her dominant eye to see through the small window if the cat was there. In the period of a second, a long cat arm struck straight out and grabbed her cheek just below the eye, holding onto it for at least two seconds. Of course she screamed and cried, but fortunately it was a superficial wound.

As the days went on, everyone fell victim to this crazy animal. It would run out of nowhere, claw and bite the crap out of us while releasing an awful low growl, and then run and hide. We were not even safe in our beds at night. It was a very, very, evil cat.

We had a Korean housekeeper named Miss Yee. She was a very patient and kind person, and would often babysit us while our parents were gone. I enjoyed the time I spent with her, but was not very fond of her cooking. Come to think about it, all she ever really made was white rice with chopped up hot dogs in it.

The cat especially relished torturing that poor woman. One day while she was cleaning the house, the cat let out one of its low grumbling growls, "Yeooogi!"

Miss Yee stood in shock. It was sitting on the other side of the living room, staring her right in the eyes.

It made its all too familiar noise again, "Yeooogi!"

She immediately got on the phone to get ahold of my mom and told her that the cat was speaking! She said that it was saying "Here!" in Korean.

Needless to say, that was all it took for my very religious mother to get that thing out of our house. I am not sure what ever happened to that cat, but if it ended up in somebody's rice bowl, it was quite all right with me.

CHAPTER 3

Tucson, Arizona

Tucson was a big change from Korea. It was actually a very welcoming change. I was very impressed with its clean, dry air and its surrounding mountains. I can still remember the first electrical storm that I witnessed there. The sun was setting spectacularly, and because Tucson was in a flat valley you could see for miles. Half the sky was on fire to the west, losing the advantage of the approaching storm. The clouds were an immense Olympus-like mountain range highlighted on the peaks from the setting sun. You could see its unpredictable nerves flaring, and cracking- illuminating the inside of its shadowy mass. Steadily moving forward it would sporadically release a cavernous growl as it consumed the valley below into its darkness. It was an amazing display of color, power, and beauty.

Our parents had enrolled us in a school called Tucson Christian School, or TCS, which taught kindergarten all the way through to the twelfth grade. It was now the beginning of the fifth grade, and my teacher was to be Mr. Maxwell. Academically, this was the beginning of a long, difficult road for me.

Mr. Maxwell was a tough teacher, but he was always fair. I remember countless nights lying awake in bed fearing that I was not going to pass his class and that I would have to be held back a grade. This was a terrifying thought—the idea of going to the

same school but not being able to move onto the next class with all of my friends.

I developed quite the mouth in the fifth grade—so much so that three times that year it earned me swats from Mr. Maxwell's infamous "Golden Rule." That was the name of his legendary paddle, which had made so many fifth graders cry. It was painted gold and had holes drilled in it.

The trick to being paddled was to not let any of the other kids see you cry. Mr. Maxwell would take the offending student into the hallway, give him two or three licks in front of another teacher as a witness, and back into class he would go. A kid named Jeff was the first one to get swats that year. I remember very well what he looked like when he returned from his spanking. It took the kid ten minutes to stop crying. He was completely demoralized and defeated.

When my turn came, as I knew it one day would, I told myself no matter how much it hurt not to let the other kids see me cry. We walked out into the hallway. My heart was beating profusely. I remember very specifically trying to keep a nice, casual stride as I got up from my desk and walked toward the hallway door. When it closed behind me, Mr. Maxwell went to the adjacent classroom to get his witness.

Returning with his witness, he asked me to bend over and place my hands on my knees. Once in the position, he asked if I understood why I was getting the swats. I answered with a simple, "Yes."

He gave me three very swift swats, and they stung incredibly. My initial reaction after the first one was to grab my butt cheeks and jump up and down from the intense stinging. I thought, "Don't cry, Brett! Don't cry, Brett! Don't you dare!"

After the third swat I asked him in a low, slow voice, "Are you done?" my head hanging towards the ground.

He replied confidently, "Yes, we are."

I raised my head and slowly turned toward both teachers, making sure my eyes locked onto each of theirs, ensuring they saw not a single fucking tear in them. The look I got in return, especially from the notorious Mr. Maxwell, was instantly gratifying.

I really did want to cry. It was extremely difficult. I wanted to cry so badly, but I knew that if I did it would be a hundred times worse letting all the kids see me broken like that.

I somehow managed to crack a smile as I walked into the classroom, casually made my way past all the staring faces, and reached my seat in the back of the class. One of the girls asked Mr. Maxwell if I had gotten swats. He disappointedly answered, "Yes, now get back to work."

From that point on, no other boy that got swats in that class cried, because we had learned that what seemed impossible was actually possible, and how something meant to humiliate and cause pain can actually inspire and encourage.

During my sixth grade Christmas vacation, our family went on a weeklong vacation to see the sights of Arizona. The trip was organized and sponsored by the base church. One of our first excursions was to drive out to an Indian reservation about two hours from the Grand Canyon.

I remember sitting on the tour bus and thinking to myself that we were literally out in the middle of the desert. Anxiously looking out the huge panel windows, I grew more and more restless to see the reservation. I knew there were not going to be teepees or headbanded warriors riding painted horses, but I was told there were kids my age, and I was excited to meet them.

As we pulled onto the reservation, I found myself in disbelief at the conditions the people were living in. There were just a few buildings scattered about. In the distance you could see the occasional home, and from what I could tell they were not much to see. The center of the reservation had three buildings from what I can remember. There was a small building that was a church, school, and community-gathering place all in one. You would have never had known it was any of those things because it looked like a pole barn. Across from it was a small clinic that was constructed from cinder blocks. Adjacent to that was a basketball court. I am not sure what the third building was but it looked like some sort of storage shed.

The church apparently had funded, or helped fund, this downtown part of the reservation, which was obviously a hit with all the local residents.

There was an Indian woman standing on the porch of the clinic as we pulled in. She was probably in her mid-thirties, and had long, thick, dark hair that had been pulled back into a ponytail. We all got off the bus, and slowly kids started to show up. One of the church leaders took the parents on a tour after speaking briefly to the Indian woman, who was now sitting in an aluminum framed fold-up beach chair.

I recall that none of the children's parents were there. The kids were much younger than me. I thought to myself that this was going to suck—I never really enjoyed playing with younger kids. Nothing was different about any of them, except that they were obviously living in poverty. We began to play with them. Tracey and another young Indian girl hit it off. They talked and acted like normal kids; they also played like normal kids.

In the distance we could hear the sound of a helicopter approaching. The church leader came running out to where we all playing and yelled, "Do you kids hear that?" The rest of the adults followed closely behind him, all with big smiles and fake expressions of surprise. "Sounds like Santa is on his way!" he exclaimed while herding stray children like cattle with his arms stretched wide, moving them away from the basketball court and towards the clinic.

The helicopter landed on the basketball court. The kids all just stood there confused as the helicopter engines wound down and the blades came to a stop. The door opened to reveal a man dressed like Santa Claus. He climbed out and turned back to the helicopter to grab a bag of presents.

Santa walked over to us with his fake beard slightly hanging off his face and gave out an uncomfortable, "Ho, ho, ho, little children."

The children stood still, looking at the guy in bewilderment.

He walked up to the middle of the group and started handing out presents.

Obviously unsure of what exactly to do, the kids looked at the woman sitting in the chair. She gave them a slight nod and they began to open their presents. Some kids played with their toys, some kids wanted somebody else's toy, and some of the kids just didn't give a shit. The whole situation was just awkward and embarrassing.

Santa finally got back in his ridiculously fancy helicopter and left. Though I could not remember it, my dad would later tell me that he rode in and flew out on the helicopter, which was actually a Blackhawk.

Not long after that, the church leader told everyone to start loading back onto the bus. I ran into the clinic to take a leak before we left for the long drive back.

When I came back out I quickly discovered that everybody was gone! Panic struck quickly. "How could they leave me?" I thought, "Calm down, Brett, calm down."

I turned to the woman in the chair, and I think she was just as shocked as I was. I wasn't in there for more than three minutes!

"Seriously, mom… you only had to count to three," I muttered as I looked down the dusty road leading away from the reservation.

Seeing my frantic state, the woman spoke to me very softly and with a thick Native American accent, "They will come back once they realize you're not on the bus."

"Do you have a phone?" I asked. She nodded yes and then asked, "Who would you like me to call?"

Unfortunately, this was long before affordable cell phones. "You could call Santa, 'cause he probably has a phone in that helicopter," I said, almost believing it. She let out a soft laugh that proved to be very contagious.

We pleasantly talked off and on for the next four hours. During the lulls in the conversation she would hum, occasionally glancing in the distance. As the hours went by, the sun started to hang low in the sky, making everything that light could touch softly resemble the color of the sunset. During the times when she hummed quietly, I would look with her out over the vast flat expanse and start to imagine my new life on the reservation. I imagined years had passed before my family ever came back to get me. When they did, they would find me in that crappy church dancing half naked around a fire with the entire tribe, and to their shock they would witness me being initiated as one of the tribesmen and becoming an Indian warrior.

That woman was very sweet. I never asked her name, and I have always regretted that. After my parents picked me up, I couldn't help but look back at her as we drove away.

The next day we made our way to the Grand Canyon. I had seen pictures of it on postcards and in schoolbooks. This was to be a daylong trip, and it did not appeal to me at all. I slept most of the drive there. In fact, I was awakened by my sister when we arrived.

"We're here, Brett, we're here!" She said as she pushed on my shoulder. I pulled my head off the windowsill and looked around. There was nothing but some trees and a parking lot. Tracey rushed out of the car.

I lethargically made my way out towards where everyone was heading. As I rounded a corner and past all the trees, I first noticed Tracey. She stood at what looked like the edge of the world. Her tiny body with her long curly red hair stood paralyzed by what she saw. It was so big that it did not even look real.

Looking back at how close the trees were to the rim, I couldn't help but wonder how many explorers or cowboys thought they were just on a walk through the woods and then fell right into the canyon. I started to walk closer to the edge to see if I could see a skeleton at the bottom. "Get back over here, Brett!" my mom demanded. I did not argue.

By the start of the seventh grade, we had finally convinced our parents that we all preferred to attend public school. Naylor Junior High was to be my induction back into normalcy, or so I thought. Bad grades, suspensions, and lots of fights would become my legacy at that school. Things at home were not much better.

Sometime close to the end of the school year, my father had come home from work and told us all that we were moving to Cairo, Egypt. Nobody, and I mean nobody, was happy about that.

Being moderately upset over this, I rode my bike to a friend's house to tell him about it. We rode our bikes around for a little bit and then sat on his front curb with the bikes laid out in the yard and talked while the sun went down. A girl named Carrie was walking home from a friend's house and stopped to talk to us. She was a pretty girl with a fair complexion and bright, thick, naturally blonde hair who was already developing breasts. She always wore dark eyeliner and red lipstick, and had a slight bad-girl attitude and reputation. I had heard from friends that she'd had her eye on me for a while.

It was now dark outside and my friend went in for dinner. Carrie asked me to walk her home. We cut through a couple of backyards to shorten the trip through the neighborhood.

She stopped in the middle of a clothesline that had a couple sheets hanging from it, blocking the residents of the house from seeing us. She turned to me and asked, "Have you ever French kissed a girl?"

I lied and said, "Of course."

The moon was already bright that night, and I watched her as she took two steps towards me. I let my bike fall to the ground and put my left hand on her hip and used my right hand to move her hair and hold the back of her head like I had seen on TV. She tasted like grape bubble gum.

When we got to her front door, she turned and smiled while wiping the bright red lipstick off my mouth. "Thanks for walking me home, Brett," she said as she walked inside.

I rode my bike home feeling like the man! Though we would talk a little before the move, we never kissed again or talked about it.

I knew I liked guys, but something about that made me feel like maybe there was hope for girls and me. Even though it was not an enjoyable experience. I felt like I had just mowed the yard, or cleaned my room without being told, something that would make one feel a kind of pride completing, but glad it was over. I also thought that because I'd actually gone through with it, it had to mean something.

In preparation for our move, our family had already packed all of our belongings and rented an apartment just off the base. My father had already flown ahead of us to Cairo. Needless to say, I made friends with all the wrong people at the apartment complex. It was chock full of kids doing bad things.

Due to my magnetic ability to attract trouble, my mother had me visiting a psychiatrist named Dr. Boles. I don't remember much about the man, except that he was really big and unkempt, and smelled like mothballs. The reason my mother had me visit with him in particular was because he was a Christian, and his treatments were done according to Christian principles.

All hell broke loose in our apartment one night. I honestly can't remember the cause. I know that my mother called the good doctor, my brother tearfully tied me up with rope, and they carried me to our car. They took me to Charter Behavioral Hospital.

It was like a hotel with no access to the outdoors, which was the worst place in the world for a kid like me. The kids occupied one wing of the hospital. There were about ten rooms on either side of the hallway and one community room by the nurse's station, which was behind a magnetically locked door. One room, one hallway, and a community room with 5 channels on the TV, that's it!

One shot of Thorazine, two escape attempts, and six weeks later (with a promise to be good), I found myself on a plane to Cairo.

CHAPTER 4

Cairo, Egypt

The flights were long and miserable. As the plane began its descent, my sister and I looked out the window to a very dismal sight. Coming in for landing we began to wonder if we were going to land on dirt, because that was all you could see. My visions of pyramids, blue skies, and a turquoise Nile River were shattered. Getting off the plane, we quickly realized this place was gross and smelled like shit.

My father met us at the airport with his driver and an armored car. We then proceeded to an apartment in Maudi, a suburb of Cairo. We would eventually move into a guarded and walled-in house once our belongings arrived from the United States.

It was nighttime, and we all found ourselves wide awake from the jet lag. My mother gave us each a giant black sleeping pill. She instructed us to go right to bed. I told her that I really needed to take a shower, and she said to be quick about it.

There was no showerhead in the bathroom by my room, so I ran a bath instead. As I slipped into the tub I could see the dust and dirt coming off my body. That was about all that I remember.

Hours later I awoke, still in the tub, shivering profusely. I was very disoriented, trying to remember what happened and where I was. Somehow I made my way to my room and crawled under the sheets butt naked feeling drunk, high, and really cold. It was not until noon the next day that any of us woke up.

Not too long after we arrived, my parents began the process of enrolling us in school. The Cairo American College was a very large school, and was guarded and gated. Unfortunately, I would not know what it would be like to go there. For some reason, I was told they would not accept my transcripts. However, my brother's and sister's transcripts worked just fine.

The following week I found myself with my parents in an armored car heading to Alexandria, which was about three hours away. I was being enrolled in an "American" boarding school. I was extremely upset over this, as I would imagine anyone would be. Before leaving me, my parents told me I could go to the bus station and catch a bus back to Cairo on the weekends. They gave me some money for it, plus some taxi fare to get from the bus station to the house, then off they went.

This school was brutal. There were only three Americans working there—the headmaster and a married couple that taught there. Unfortunately, none of them were my teachers. I was the only American student, although there was a Canadian brother and sister that lived across the hall from me. The girl was in ninth grade and really helped me with my math. This proved to be very convenient since my math teacher spoke half in English and the other half in Arabic. The sadist spoke perfect English. She knew that I was the only American in the class, that I was the only kid who did not speak Arabic, and that I was not a Muslim. She was always partial to the Muslim students, and she relished setting me apart. There were numerous occasions when I am sure I was the butt of a joke. Often, after she had said something in Arabic and sent me a cold glance, the class broke out in laughter.

Oddly enough, the math teacher was also our physical education teacher. Her favorite activity for us was swimming.

She would have us swim laps for about thirty minutes, and then at the end of the session would have us swim underwater for as long as we could without coming up for air. She would then note our performance on her clipboard.

Her son, Mohammed, was in the tenth grade. He was a big guy, clearly no stranger to a gym—or to steroids, for that matter. He was in incredible shape. He would always win everything, and was an especially fast swimmer.

As the year went on, I focused really hard on trying to beat him in the water. He always managed to win, much to the delight of his mother. While on a lunch break towards the end of fall, Mohammed was hanging out with his minions and started poking fun at me, saying how I would never be able to beat him.

I replied, "Maybe, but I bet I can swim underwater longer than you." Mohammed did not like that I had called him out in front of his followers. The pool had been closed for about a week because it had gotten too cold to swim, but that did not stop us from grabbing our swim trunks and making our way to the pool.

Mohammed's mother had gotten wind of this and actually opened the gate for us. It was like a boxing match. I was at one corner with the two Canadians, and Mohammed was at the other with his cronies. His mother would occasionally look up at me with a disdainful smirk. I disliked her almost as much as I disliked her son.

Mohammed was the first to go. The pool was twenty-five meters long. His mother whispered something in his ear. You could see her breath in the cold air. He jumped up and down a couple times to try and warm himself up and then jumped into the pool. When he came up from under the water his mother said something to him very sternly in Arabic. He nodded, took two deep breaths, and on the third loud inhale submerged himself and pushed off the wall.

He glided under the water. His breaststroke was perfect as he made his way to the other end of the pool, constantly remaining about two feet from the surface. He touched the wall and started on his way back.

The furthest any of the students had ever seen somebody swim underwater was when Mohammed, after one swim practice, he swam a whole fifty meters. At the time, none of us could believe it.

As he approached the fifty-meter mark, we could tell he was starting to run out of air. His stroke became faster and faster. All I could think was, "Please come up, please come up." I knew I had a chance at doing fifty meters; I had come close to it before in the past.

Mohammed touched the wall and then turned to head back. He pushed off violently and swam vigorously underwater until he reached a buoyed rope that ran across the middle of the pool, separating the shallow end from the deep. Mohammed had swum two and a half lengths of the pool. He arose to find his mother content and his friends clapping.

Now it was my turn. I turned and looked at the Canadian girl as I took off my jacket.

She told me very calmly, "All you have to do is not come up."

Somehow that brought me no comfort. I took a breath and enjoyed my last second of warmth and jumped into the pool. The water was so cold that it took my breath away. I stood up, wrapped my arms around myself, and said, "Wow... that is freeeezing!" I thought I would get at least one laugh or chuckle. I didn't get shit.

I turned and looked at the end of the pool and started taking slow, deep breaths. I let the sounds of cars, birds, and even the breeze rustling through the trees comfort me. It did not take long for the mumbled chatter from Mohammed and his friends to fade away. Soon I felt alone; I felt a peace and solitude move over me.

I took four or five very short breaths to make myself hyperventilate, followed by a long deep breath to take in as much air as my lungs could possibly allow. Then I submerged myself under the water and pushed off the wall. Feeling that the air in my lungs was starting push me back to the surface, I began to swim down to bottom, where the pressure made me feel less buoyant. It was so quiet and peaceful under the surface, the water was crystal clear and the sunbeams shimmered on the rippled surface, creating a calming light show on the bottom of the pool.

I made it to the end with no problems, and then turned to push off the wall. The moment after I pushed off I felt the strong desire to return to the surface. I pushed on. As I reached the halfway point I felt a familiar panic come over me, causing me to swim faster.

I had now made it to the fifty meter mark. This was officially the longest I had ever been underwater. I turned and kicked myself off the wall as hard as I could. I could see the finish line, and it was agonizing. The buoyed line was just feet away.

As fast as the panic had come over me, it suddenly dissipated. I started to become calm again. By the time I hit the seventy-five meter mark I was completely tranquil. Returning to the shallow end, a sense of well-being flowed over me. The water felt somehow warm, and I was relaxed.

As I swam under the line my vision started to fade. My heart was beating slowly, but when it did beat it was loud enough that I could hear it.

When I touched the wall after swimming one hundred meters underwater, my vision was all but gone. I came to the surface and took a huge breath, followed by heavy, rapid breathing. My body was trembling, my lungs felt almost collapsed. As my vision returned, I looked to the Canadian girl, who smiled pleasantly and gave me the thumbs up.

There was no clapping. In fact it was so quiet you could hear a pin drop. In the distance was Mohammed walking back to the locker room. Judging by how far away he was, he must have left after I'd broken his record.

The fact that no one clapped for me actually made me quite content. I had beaten that arrogant motherfucker in front of his friends and his mother, and that was all I needed. Mohammed never spoke to me again.

This moment in time became very important to me—it was when I started to realize that I had something special. Though I did not have any superpowers, I was beginning to discover that I had something better. I was discovering my own willpower.

A couple weeks later I headed back to Cairo for the weekend on a Jinga bus, a contraption which looks like a bunch of beer cans and shiny crap sewn together into the shape of a bus. It was just like every other time I took the bus home. It was crammed full, the people stunk really bad, and the occasional farm animal always kept things interesting. After getting off I walked over to a taxi stand and got a ride home.

Upon arriving at my parent's, my brother and sister were the first ones to greet me when I walked in the door. It had been two weeks since I had last come home—I had opted to spend the previous weekend at school to avoid the miserable bus ride. My brother began to tell me about a séance that he and his friends had the weekend prior. Though I was not there I would go on to hear about it for many years after. Apparently my mother was downstairs and could tell there was evil happening in the house. Needless to say, Marc spent the week at home without friends.

My father was on a trip somewhere that weekend, and Marc asked me if I wanted to sneak out of the house and go on a Faluka, or party boat, ride on the Nile that night. Of course I agreed. We snuck out and met up with all of his friends, getting moderately drunk on the three-hour ride.

We tried to sneak back in the house, but my mother had discovered we were not in our rooms and was waiting by the first floor entrance. There was a couch near the front door of that freaking castle, and she had positioned herself on it to catch us coming back. My brother was the first to notice her, and he immediately turned to me and pushed his index finger over his lips to signal me to be as quiet as possible. I looked over, and as luck would have it she had fallen asleep. We knew we were going to get in trouble for sneaking out, but if we got busted drinking it would be ten times worse—especially after Marc had tried raising the dead or talking to Satan or whatever it was he'd done the week before.

As we crept towards the spiral staircase just beyond my mother's sofa, her snoring instantly stopped. She rose up quickly, almost like a vampire from the coffin, and growled, "Where have you two been?"

My brother belligerently responded, "Out with friends."

She looked at me and asked very sternly, "Have you been drinking?"

My brother responded, "No."

She then indicated with her index finger to come closer and asked me to blow on her. I did, and to my amazement she said, "You pass, go to bed!"

As I walked slowly up the stairs, I turned to watch my brother's test. Immediately after he'd blown on her face she angrily told him, "You fail! You're in big trouble, mister. Wait 'till your dad hears about this!"

I left the next day to go back. For the first time I was very thankful for being shipped off to a boarding school. I wasn't really sure what happened to my brother, but somehow, for the first time ever, I'd managed to sneak one by my parents.

Weeks went by and I had befriended a kid named Kasala. Kasala was from Zambia and his father served as a consul in the Zambian Embassy. Kasala was a very rich kid. His father would pick him up from school in a brand new Mercedes. He also gave him a moped to drive around town in. This moped was almost the death of me on several occasions. For the record, never drive a damn moped on an Egyptian highway during rush hour!

About three months before the end of the school year, Kasala told me that he had scored some weed. He asked me if I wanted to go up on the roof and smoke it with him. Having never smoked weed before, and being very curious, I agreed. We smoked the whole joint quickly to lesson our chances of being caught. Not feeling much of anything, we climbed down and went back to our room. By the time we got there it had hit me. I was laughing uncontrollably. I was laughing so much and so loudly that the dorm parent who lived down the hall came to my room and asked me to keep it down. He was probably no stranger to Mary Jane himself; once he looked at me he knew exactly what I had been doing. The next day I was on a bus back to Cairo for good.

I can't say that I was upset; in fact, I was a little relieved. I hated that school. The only problem was that my parents were unaware of what had happened because the phones were very sketchy and they could not get through. I was not looking forward to explaining it to them.

The days leading up to summer were painful. I was stuck in a house with my mother, and spent most of my time in my room. My arguments with my family got worse. The distance between us grew greater and greater.

During this time, however, one occasion stands out very well against the general malaise. My brother and father were in the kitchen talking. They were talking about Navy SEALs. Not having any idea of what a Navy SEAL was, I joined in and asked. My father explained that he had heard about this group of guys when he was in Vietnam, but that he did not really know exactly what they did, aside from being really good shooters and divers.

It turns out that a group of Navy SEALs had come to the American Embassy in Cairo. My dad was a full bird colonel in the Air Force, and they would not let anybody, even him, see these men. They wouldn't even tell him why they were there.

This fascinated me. My mind ran rampant with ideas, and I wondered what these guys could be doing that not even my father was allowed to know about it—or why he couldn't even see their faces, for that matter. The seed was planted.

That summer my best friend's brother, who was also a friend of my brother's, overdosed on heroin. His friends dumped his body in the desert because they got scared and did not know how to handle it. The Egyptian police found the body a couple days later and immediately went looking for the culprits.

I remember very clearly my dad rushing home to ask us if we knew anything about it. We were in shock. We had no idea. I think my dad could tell by our expressions that we were sincere. His efforts were meant to keep us from getting raped in an Egyptian jail somewhere.

I felt incredibly bad for the guy's dad. My friend would later tell me how his dad had locked himself in his brother's room for days after he found out about his son's death. Something about that boy's death resonated with me. A sense of its permanence was magnified by his father's actions.

I knew his father really loved him, and I was jealous of that.

CHAPTER 5

Austin, Texas

It was not long after that we all found ourselves on a plane heading to Austin, Texas—the capital of the Lone Star State, the state that I would come to know as home. Once again, I soon found myself at another treatment center for delinquent children—only this time it was different. My parents had tried everything from behavioral hospitals to boarding schools. They were fed up with my shit and truly wanted me out of their house long-term. They found the perfect place in Liberty Hill, Texas, a place called Merridell Achievement Center. It was a boy's ranch located out in the middle of nowhere, about an hour's drive from Austin. I would spend the next two years there.

I remember my first day very well. After driving up a long road to the three trailers that made up the administrative offices, my parents left me standing by the car with my suitcase. They walked into one of the trailers. I was wearing a pair of acid-washed jeans that were littered with holes and pegged at the bottom. I had on a white Ocean Pacific T-shirt and a pair of docksiders on my feet. I vividly remember standing very nervously, waiting in the sun for my parents to come out again as kids walked by looking at me. I was very scared of this place.

A good-looking, slightly overweight, forty-something man with short, dark, and curly Caesar-like hair walked out of the trailer my parents were in. He had a skateboard in his hand. I watched as he placed it on the sidewalk and skated over to me. "Do you sail?" he asked, very eager for my response.

"I probably wouldn't be here if I did." I could tell he found that amusing. "Why are you asking me that?" I responded.

"Because you're wearing sailing shoes. I like to sail," he told me. He asked my name and tried to make small talk. Before he skated back off to the trailer he asked why I was there.

My response was, "Family problems, I guess."

I would later come to know that man as Doc. He was the psychiatrist who founded, ran, and owned the boy's ranch.

The ranch was separated into seven different groups. A group was made up of about eight boys. We all lived in cabins in the woods, all connected with trails with which I would become intimately familiar with over the years. Our group was called the Roadrunners, and our cabin was the closest to the cafeteria. I always felt bad for the Bobcats, since they were the youngest kids and their cabin was the furthest away. It took them about twenty minutes to get to the cafeteria.

Each of the groups was assigned a case supervisor. This person would be involved with their treatment, and often attended their family meetings. Case supervisors were also in charge of the staff that would be assigned to a particular group.

Staff members would very rarely work with a different group unless there was a staffing shortage and none or very few of the kids in his group were in trouble. They became very close to, and almost territorial with, their groups.

School was a privilege; it was not forced on any kid. The only problem was that if you did not want to go to school you would have to work while other kids were studying.

The boy's ranch was also pretty harsh on the kids that sexually acted out. The staff never kept it a secret from other kids, so it became public knowledge. It was one of the things I really hated about the place. All that really did was unnecessarily out the gay, bi, trans, or just confused kids and give the other kids ammunition to bully or shame them. Obviously, kids having sex was a bad idea. But it could have been handled better.

The place was unlike anything that I had ever seen or heard of before. It had its own, very bizarre, rules.

Kids who had socks on their hands had gotten in trouble for hitting somebody or getting into a fight.

Kids who had a three-foot string around their wrist attached to one of the staff had gotten into some kind of trouble that required them to be supervised all the time. If you broke the string it gave the staff the green light to "sit on you." They would pin you to the ground on your stomach and hold your hands behind your back. They would do this until they felt comfortable letting you up. It usually involved a lot of talking about feelings.

Personal Restriction was the same thing as being on the string, except there was no string. You had to stay within three feet of the staff at all times.

PJ's were the clothing issued to kids who had tried to run away. They consisted of a white T-shirt and very unattractive gray sweatpants. Any personal clothes would get locked up.

Some kids wore signs around their necks. This usually meant the kid had a different problem—cussing or stealing, for example.

You were never allowed to talk about drugs without one of the staff being present. This was a very serious offense; the punishment was a spot on the TORI club. This stood for Turkeys On Ranch Indefinitely. Once in this club there was no getting out of it… ever! It meant that you would never be able to go on day trips with the rest of the kids; it meant that you had to work on the weekends every Saturday and Sunday morning. More importantly, you would never be allowed to go on weekend home visits to see your family. You were on that damn ranch till

the day your treatment was done, you turned 18, or you died…
whichever came first.

A TORI slip was when someone said a word or phrase that
could be perceived as drug-related, even if it was not intended
that way. For example: "That kid is such a trip, he loves climbing trees." The use of the word "trip" could be referencing
LSD. If someone said something like this, he would immediately have to find a staff member, wherever they might be, and
report it so that it would not become a TORI secret. Failure to
do this would mean a spot on the TORI club.

To find freedom from any one of these restrictions, you
would have to work. The work was never easy. The more severe
the crime, the more severe the punishment—clearing trails,
pulling weeds, etc.

My first family counseling came the week after I arrived. I
remember being very upset that my parents had left me there.
I watched them walk from their car, as if they had no cares in
the world. I could see how happy they were without me. I could
actually see it; they left a trail of rainbows behind them.

Needless to say, our meeting did not go well. It ended
with me telling the case supervisor and family counselor, right
in front of my parents, that I did not want to see or talk to them
for at least six months. I thought that somehow this would
make them regret their decision to leave me here.

To my shock and dismay, the family counselor agreed with
me. I turned to my father; I specifically remember the look on
his face. I saw his eyes break from a stern glare, revealing relief.
My mother, on the other hand, remained somber and quiet. It
would be six months before we talked again.

When we bitterly said our goodbyes after that, the invisi-
ble force that holds one to his family would forever be gone for
me. It was a hard and painful truth for a fourteen-year-old boy
to understand. This isn't saying that I didn't love my family—

far from it. I just love them individually and in unique ways. It would not be until I was thirty-seven that I again felt what being in a real family, in every sense of the word, was like.

It did not take me long after that to find myself out of the classroom, wearing PJ's, socks on my hands, a sign around my neck, a broken string around my wrist, and a staff member sitting on top of me holding my hands behind my back. I had made it to the ranch's rock bottom in record time.

I would like to say that over the next six months I worked off all those restrictions and managed to keep all that crap off of me. In reality, as soon as I worked one thing off, I would find a way to get something new put on me. But towards the end of my time there, I would manage to go a month or so without having to wear any of the ranch's accessories. This was a major accomplishment for me at the time.

Family time never really worked out after those first six months. We would never truly communicate with each other again. We just went through the motions. Even after I left the ranch to live with my family again and finish high school it was always awkward and turbulent. There were moments when things felt right, but they were always fleeting.

During my two-plus years at the boy's ranch I became friends with a number of different kids who came in and out of that place. Jeremy was from south Texas, along the coast, and spoke very highly of surfing. We had become very good friends, even in the short time that he was there.

Both of us being very upset with our lots in life, we had decided that we were going to run away from the ranch together. Our plan was rather impulsive—we talked about it one day at lunch and planned to run away that night as soon it was lights out.

Running away from the ranch was not a very difficult thing to do. The doors to the cabin were never locked. Additionally, it was not hard to outrun most of the staff if they chased you. There was just one fence that surrounded the perimeter of the ranch itself, and it was just a short barbed wire fence. Its only purpose was to keep cattle from entering the property.

Our plan was to grab our clothes and whatever else we could, and put them in a pillowcase on our bed. We would wait for the person on duty to turn off the lights and make her way to the small TV room located on the far left-hand side of the cabin. We would make our exodus out the door in the middle of the cabin that divided the four sets of bunk beds. The end plan was to find our way to south Texas to live with a friend of his who was "cool."

The moments leading up to that point were terrifying. I kept thinking, "What if Jeremy does not run out of the cabin with me?" Time was going by very slowly. I watched when, as if in slow motion, the staff member turned out the lights and made her way to the TV room.

As soon as she closed the TV room door, we both jumped out of our beds and sprinted the few steps to the exit. I was coming from the left side, and he was coming from the right. Our eyes had not yet adjusted to the darkness, so we comically ran into each other right in front of the door. Frantically fumbling for the door, we somehow managed to get it open. As we stumbled into the moonless night, we found ourselves struggling to see the gravel road that led up to the cabin. We ran for the first few minutes based off memory.

Eventually, we found ourselves at the barbed wire fence. We made our way over it and started crossing the neighboring field. The staff member must have phoned the on-duty supervisor because just then, headlights from one of the ranch trucks flared around toward our cabin in an attempt to find us.

It did not take long for us to slow to a walk due to the exhaustion of our initial escape. My eyes had started adjusting to the dark night, and I noticed steam was coming off our heads. Jeremy did not have his pillowcase and was wearing shorts. It was cold out, and I asked, "Dude, did you drop your bag?"

"I forgot to grab it!" he whispered sternly.

I looked at him through my breath in the frigid air and said, "Oh, fuck."

I had brought one pair of sweatpants and one sweatshirt, which I was already wearing at this point. He had on a T-shirt and shorts. We decided that he would take the T-shirt that I had on under the sweatshirt so he could double them up. He would also take the sweatpants because I had shorts on underneath. Our plan was to rotate who wore the sweatpants and who wore the sweatshirt through the night as needed to stay warm.

As we made our way through the various fields leading to the nearest intersection, I could make out large mounds of dirt scattered about, with the occasional tree. When we got to the first one, I told Jeremy to hold up while I tied my shoe. I stuck my foot on the mound and began to lean over. The mound suddenly moved and made a loud, deep groaning sound. I immediately jumped back and landed on my butt, letting out a loud, "Ahhhh!" Just then, all the mounds got to their feet—they were actually giant black cows. Jeremy was in just as much shock as I was. We ran to the nearest fence, thinking they would stampede us.

At the intersection of the first road we came to was a gas station. We decided that we needed to get some matches for a fire because it was so cold. We knew that the ranch had probably called the local police station, so we needed to make this happen fast. I gave him the sweatshirt while he went inside, in hopes of making him look more normal. He was gone for about ten minutes.

Returning to see me visibly cold, he handed me the sweatshirt and said, "They gave me some matches, but we should probably get as far away from here as possible. One of the ladies in the convenience store was looking at me weird."

We left, running for a few minutes to get warm, and then walked again. We did this for hours, staying about a hundred yards off the side of the highway.

There were very few cars driving by at that time of night, but when one did we would hit the ground and lay flat between the muddy tilled rows in the fields we were navigating.

Eventually, we found ourselves under a highway bridge next to a large creek. We both immediately went looking for firewood. We decided to start a fire under the bridge, where we would try to sleep that night.

It did not take long for the fire to get started, and it was awesome and warm. The problem was that it lit up the entire area surrounding the bridge. We knew we were going to have to put it out because it was visible to passing cars. It broke our hearts to put that fire out. We eventually found a grassed area near the bridge and we laid down to try and sleep.

Soon it had gotten so cold that Jeremy said, "Dude, I am not being a fag, but we are going to have lay up next to each other."

We attempted that for about fifteen minutes, without much luck. At this point we were both shivering like jackhammers next to each other. I'm not sure who came up with the idea, but we then attempted to fit ourselves into the sweatshirt and the sweatpants at the same time. I imagine we looked extremely ridiculous as we both tried to get into one set of clothes. After a few curse words thrown at each other, and a couple of falls to the ground, we were able to somehow make it happen.

By this point in my life there was no doubt I was one hundred percent gay. Though Jeremy was an eye-catching kid, I was in no way attracted to him. At the time, I liked older guys. I valued the friendship and certainly did not want to do anything that would threaten it. It is very rare for me to be sexually attracted to anybody who is straight… which Jeremy definitely was.

We woke up to the sun starting to lighten the sky. As we climbed out of our makeshift shelter, the first thing I noticed was how dirty we were and how stretched out our clothes had become. We made our way to the creek and got some water to drink and wash our faces and hands with. After I adjusted my blown-out sweatshirt by tucking it into my shorts and he tied his pants and tucked their bottoms into his socks, we decided to follow the creek upstream to see where it took us. It would also keep us away from the road.

A few hours later we came across a deer blind up in a tree. It was starting to get warm, and we both were very tired. We decided to climb up it and get some sleep. It was not very big, but it blocked the wind and was rather warm. We fell asleep immediately, and slept for a couple of hours.

We awoke to the sound of a man yelling in the distance, "I know you kids are out here!" We both jumped up immediately and as quick as we could climbed down and ran. The voice was coming from downstream. The stream was in the middle of farming fields, but trees had grown up alongside the creek, which provided us concealment.

We ran for about fifteen minutes and stopped just before a break in the trees. Jeremy went to get a drink from the creek while I looked to the other side where the trees had started to grow again. I could not see anybody or anything. It was about fifty meters to cross the open field. As I peered intently, I heard a loud, "Get the fuck back over here!" I turned around and saw Jeremy running frantically towards me. "It's the cops, Brett… Run!" We both started to run together across the gap, I turned around and saw the police officer in hot pursuit on foot not far behind us. I could tell that we were running faster than him because the second time I looked back I saw we were getting farther away from him. Only this time he had his gun in his hand.

"Stop right fucking now, goddammit!" he yelled, obviously out of breath. Just then a loud, thunderous crack filled the air. He had just fired his gun!

I immediately stopped. Jeremy turned around and said, "Come on, Brett!"

"Fuck that! He is going to shoot us!" I replied and raised my hands in the air.

"He is not going to shoot you," Jeremy said. I stood still and just looked at him. Jeremy gave me a look of disappointment and then he raised his hands.

The cop ran up to Jeremy first and put handcuffs on him, and told me not to move a muscle. He then grabbed me and had us walk through the field to a dirt tracker road that ran down the middle of it. While we were walking he got on his radio and told somebody that he'd "got 'em." Moments later, a police car pulled up next to us. A skinny, older officer got out and put his handcuffs on me.

"You boys are on private property," the older officer said in a thick Texas accent. "The owner doesn't take to trespassers. You boys from that place in Liberty Hill?" he inquired. "Well, today is not your lucky day, is it?" He laughed, and then let out a deep smoker's cough while putting us in the back of the patrol car.

We returned to the ranch. Everyone was standing motionless as we got out of the car, muddy and handcuffed. One of the staff members went up to the officers and talked to them beyond my earshot. The officer returned, un-cuffed us, and walked us over to him. The staff member was our case supervisor. He looked at us calmly and looked back at the officer, "Thank you, officer," he said.

The officer walked away, and our case supervisor said with a warm smile, "You guys must be hungry." That was literally the last thing I expected to hear out of his mouth. "By the looks of you two, I'd bet you boys had an interesting night." He chuckled as he walked us to the chow hall.

The punishment was rough. It involved many hours of manual labor building and clearing walking trails between the cabins. Jeremy managed to get his shit together not long after that and went home.

There would be several more unsuccessful escape attempts. Embarrassing as it is to admit, mine and Jeremy's was the best planned. My other attempts would be a direct result of becoming so overwhelmed in the moment that I would say, "Screw it, I'm outta here!" and take off running toward the fence. No water, no clothes, no food, just a boy running with no direction.

Becoming so overwhelmed was largely due to my borderline personality disorder. The best way I know how to explain it is how Doc explained it to me. He told me one day that I put things into two pots—a good pot and a bad pot. Any situation or person would end up in one of the two pots. There was nothing in-between. An imbalance to either side would overwhelm me. For example, if I felt something or someone belonged in the good pot I would feel like a million bucks for a while, until things started going in the bad pot. The bad pot would cause me to have a type of anxiety and paranoia that is very difficult to describe. I would get incredibly frustrated very fast and often get violent or abusive. Think of it like what happens to Dr. Bruce Banner when he turns into the Incredible Hulk. He knows he is about to turn and can feel it. He even tries to warn the people he cares about. Once he turns, though, there is little he can do. It also works that way in the opposite direction. Instead of turning into the Hulk, you turn into Happy Man. Happy Man may not sound bad, but it is incredibly distracting. You become so happy that it is all you can think about. Losing that happiness adds to the bad pot. All roads seem to lead right back to the bad pot. It is a frustrating cycle.

As I grew older, I discovered a way to control the two extremes. The easiest, not-so-healthy way was to drink alcohol or take prescription drugs when the familiar anxiety would start to set in. However, my preferred and most effective method is to push my body to physical exhaustion with exercise. Having an exhausted body and a clear mind would allow me to mitigate whatever was causing the extreme anxiety.

I have accepted that this will be a lifelong struggle for me. Though it gets easier the older I get, every once in awhile if I forget to hit the gym or go for a run, it becomes very apparent to those around me that I am not myself.

Looking back, I am very thankful for the ranch. I know that it was what I needed to grow. I had people there who could be like a father to me. I learned how to wrestle, play football, pass a class in school, and even how to build a stupid trail. I had grown close to those kids and staff, and I was sad to go... but not too sad.

CHAPTER 6

The Closet

Walking into the living room I called out, "Mom, are you home?"

I heard my father's voice, loudly coming from their bedroom, "Brett! Get back here!"

"Oh shit," I thought to myself, "What could I have possibly done now?"

As I entered their bedroom, my mother was draped across the bed with her head in her hands, sobbing. I looked up to see my dad standing angrily in his dress uniform. He looked me straight in the eyes and asked me point blank, "Brett, are you a homosexual?"

That question completely caught me off guard. Shaken and frightened, I replied, "What? No."

My mother raised her head off of the bed and said, "I heard your conversation with some guy named..." just then she waved her hand down at the wrist and said flamboyantly, "Pat. Homosexuals go straight to hell, Brett," she warned.

My father stood very rigidly. He was beyond angry; I could see it in his eyes. Every second that passed I could feel something unfamiliar happen. Though I was there and in the moment, I somehow found a way to make myself numb inside. This was a tool I had just at that moment discovered to actively communicate while somehow detaching my emotions—especially shame—from the situation.

"I am not going to have you infecting this family with those diseases!" my father proclaimed.

I can't remember much of the conversation after that. I am sure there was arguing, yelling, threatening, etc. However, I did confess to being gay.

Okay, let's go back a bit. While I was a sophomore in high school, my parents bought a computer with dial-up capability. It did not take me long to discover a thing called bulletin boards. Keep in mind that this was before the World Wide Web. I had discovered a bulletin board system where gay people posted personal ads with their phone numbers.

It did not take me long to build up the courage to call one of them. I spoke to a man who told me his name was John. We started talking about what we looked like, our hobbies—just stuff to get to know each other better. We had several phone conversations over the course of the next couple of weeks.

After one conversation, he asked if I wanted to meet him somewhere. The idea was so intriguing, but felt almost deviant. So of course I agreed. He picked me up at a gas station just off the base. We ended up going to his apartment. The conversation was awkward the whole time we drove because we both knew where this was leading. His car was very clean but had the smell of some crappy car wash fragrance like vanilla.

His apartment was neat and very clean. As we talked on his couch, I noticed a picture on his wall just to the left of the front door. It was one of those pictures that actually have two pictures in it, right next to each other. They were identical; it was the same black and white picture of an oddly plain male face printed twice. The only difference was that above one picture was written "Straight" and above the other, "Gay."

As predicted, the conversation got heavy, and one thing led to another. I lost my virginity that night. It was nothing like I had hoped it would be. In fact it was extremely awkward, uncomfortable, and anticlimactic. We would never talk or see each other again, and I was very okay with that.

When I got home I immediately jerked off and went to bed. I felt a strange void inside, like I had somehow found and erased a subconscious place were my parents' beliefs and views had surreptitiously taken up residence. It was very confusing for me at the time, and made sleep a difficult thing. Oddly enough, when I woke up the next morning… it did not bother me anymore. In fact, I felt great, and very content—almost as if it was an affliction or burden that I had finally gotten rid of.

As my senior year was approaching, I had found a summer job working as a bagger at the base commissary after being let loose from summer school (an every-summer thing for me). I worked off of tips, and the tips were usually really good. I could make up to twenty dollars an hour on a good day.

With money in my pocket and it being a Friday night, I drove to downtown Austin and came across a gay bar by complete accident. It was called the 404 due to its location on Fourth Street. The doorman didn't even ask me my age or ask to see my driver's license. I walked in, and from then on I was hooked. I could not believe that there were so many other people like me in this town. I walked around the bar completely mystified. I was extremely afraid to talk to anyone. In my mind, no matter who it might be, it would inevitably end up getting back to my friends or my parents that I was here. I did not stay long that night because I had a curfew, but I knew that I would be back.

The next weekend could not come fast enough. I was so excited about this new place. I arrived a little early. Well, let's just say there were only about ten people in the bar. I came to find out the bar was an eighteen and over place, but if you looked old enough it really did not matter; they would still serve you alcohol. Even the guys and girls that were obviously underage could go to a bar in the basement and drink, as long as they kept their drinks downstairs.

It was not long before a guy named Pat came up to talk to me. Pat was a little older then I was. He was a slender-built black man who was very well groomed. He actually reminded me of a male version of Grace Jones. Pat and I hung out all night.

It was getting close to midnight and I knew I had to get home. Obviously being in no shape to drive, Pat offered to drive my car and let me crash at his house. So off to his apartment we went.

That night it is still a little hazy to me, but I remember us talking at some point about how I thought he was a good-looking guy, but that he was not my type. I vaguely remember him feeling the same way about me. As a side note, I felt very little attraction to feminine guys, and aside from the penis between his legs he was all woman. I liked Pat. He was funny, fun to hang out with, and unabashedly proud of who he was. I admired that about him.

The next morning I slowly and painfully awoke in a room with only a mattress on the floor. Clothes were scattered about. I sat up and looked next to me, and there was Pat, still sleeping, wearing nothing but a leopard print thong. I lifted the covers to see if I was wearing any underwear. "Oh, thank God. That is a good sign," I thought to myself, looking at my tighty-whities.

I started to get up and look for my clothes when Pat awoke. He asked, "What are you doing?"

"Uhhh, getting dressed," I said, pulling my pants up. "Did we…"

Pat immediately began to laugh. "No, stupid." My relief was immense.

Pat and I became really good friends after that. He introduced me to a guy named Jason, who would become my secret boyfriend for a few months. Due to Pat's obvious attention-grabbing wardrobe and mannerisms, our friendship would remain a secret as well. Looking back, I always hated that I treated him like that. I know it is no excuse, but I was just so terrified about anybody finding out about this secret life I had.

Halfway through my senior year, Pat called the house one night. I always knew when it was him calling, so I would be quick to answer the phone before anybody in the house could pick up on another line. Somehow, my mother was able to pick up the phone in her room before I answered in the kitchen. I would always give it about a second to see if I could hear that unmistakable click of another receiver.

As I remember, the conversation was all about this Jason, and how he and I had made out for about an hour at his house. I remember telling Pat how I thought it was so cool that Jason's parents did not mind. The phone call lasted about twenty minutes altogether.

The next day after school I immediately went to the commissary and bagged groceries for about two hours. Afterwards I went home. I remember very well walking into the house and how quiet everything was. Usually my mother was preparing dinner, and my sister would be watching TV or doing homework somewhere nearby the kitchen. Not today. This was the day my identity was ambushed in my parents' bedroom.

After the confrontation, I was asked to leave, with specific instructions to never return. My brother drove me to a cheap hotel that was just about a half mile away from my high school. He gave me some money that my parents had instructed him to pass along. I think it was three hundred dollars.

I looked for some kind of consolation from him. I know that he was probably just as shocked as my parents were when he found out. He was in survival mode, he just wanted to do his job and leave. It was a lot for him to take in.

As he drove away, it felt like a piece of my being was still in that car being ripped away from me. I had never seen my brother like this. He did not even want to look at me. My hero, my role model… my brother couldn't even look at me.

I was ashamed of who I was, and ashamed of my name. I was a completely broken human being.

My sister Tracey was the only one who already knew. I had confided in her months prior. She never cared about it at all. In fact, she always did her best to make me feel okay about it. I would hold onto and cherish that acceptance for the rest of my life.

As I lay on the pullout couch in the run-down room I thought long and hard about what my next step was going to be. So many thoughts came to my mind... so many ideas, both good and bad. Self-loathing, darkness, hovered in the shadows and corners of that room, patiently waiting for something, anything to grab ahold of and give it strength. It was a presence I had known my whole life. Never before had it been this close. Never before did it have this strength and reason.

A war was fought in that room. Morning finally succeeded the longest night of my life up to that point. As sunlight broke through the cracks in the curtains- it would not rest on ruin, but on a changed boy, ready to replace old prayers with new ones.

The next day I got a job at a Subway that was right near the high school. It was a quarter mile from the apartment and I could get away with eating there for free. Things were starting to look up, especially when I eventually found my way back into my parents' house and their good graces for a little while before leaving the house for good. School was over, and by some miracle of God (seriously), I graduated in summer school.

Years later, my parents would start the long process of getting a divorce. My father would fall in love with a younger woman and integrate himself into another family. The relationship that I'd had with them would slowly change. My relationship with my mother would grow to become one that was founded on a mutual respect for each other's beliefs and views, although we never agreed with each other. There is nothing that I would not do for her, and she has demonstrated countless times that there is nothing that she wouldn't do for me. She will always be my mother.

There would be many important phone calls and conversations that I would have with my father. However, they would slowly dwindle to an obligatory call on holidays and the occasional birthday. We do not speak to each other like a father and son, nor do we pretend that our relationship exists on that plane. He remains a very intelligent man whose company from time to time I enjoy. I will always love him.

I had enlisted in the United States Navy and I was somehow determined to become a Navy SEAL. I was going to prove to the world that this "faggot" would accomplish what tens of thousands of straight men had failed to do.

The morning I headed off to boot camp I woke up fully packed and ready to go. My father took off work to drive me to see my mom, who was now teaching at a Christian school not far from the house. I remember saying goodbye and giving her a really long hug, I could feel her body start to tremble in my arms. As I got back in the truck I looked back to see her standing out in front of the school, crying. She was holding her hand over her mouth watching me drive away.

When we arrived at the departures side of the airport, my dad hopped out of the truck and grabbed my suitcase from the bed. As he handed it to me his voice cracked and he said, "You can do this, Brett."

I nodded and looked him in his eyes. We stared at each other for about a second and then he grabbed me by my shoulders and, in a rare moment, pulled me in for a hug.

That day marked the end of a very difficult nineteen years for all of us. It had been a long road leading up to that point. This is not to say that our family did not have good times along the way. We shared moments, but that house never came close to feeling like a home, and it was time for me to find one.

CHAPTER 7

Great Lakes, Illinois

I had just watched Full Metal Jacket not two weeks before, and the beginning of that movie played over in my head as I flew into Chicago. There was a young Army private sitting directly behind me on the flight. The plane was half empty, so I made my way back so I could talk to him.

I introduced myself and explained to him that I was on my way to Navy boot camp. Apparently, he had just finished Army boot camp a couple months prior. He explained that it really wasn't that hard, and related it to being in a home economics class that never seemed to end. The home economics classes that I took in high school were always how to cook or balance a checkbook. I guess he noticed the puzzled look on my face, so he explained, "Relax, dude. It's eight weeks of making beds, folding clothes, and learning how to march. You would pretty much have to be an idiot to fuck it up."

I was given specific instructions to find the USO office in the airport. When we landed I made my way there. An older, out of shape sailor in uniform was sitting behind a desk and pointed me to a sign-in sheet. I filled it out and looked up to him as if to ask what to do next. He just pointed his finger to a waiting room full of luggage and other guys and girls.

We eventually made our way on a chartered bus to Great Lakes Naval Station, which was located north of Chicago on Lake Michigan.

We pulled up in front of a large building where a sailor in uniform was standing patiently. The bus doors opened and he walked into the bus. This was the point at which I thought—when I am sure most of us thought—the yelling was going to begin. I was just waiting for the, "Get the fuck off this bus, you pieces of shit! Move! Move! MOVE!"

That never happened.

The sailor simply told us to get off the bus and form a line with our bags in front of the door. We did, and then walked inside, staying in a single-file line in front of a large counter. We approached the counter and one at a time told the civilian sitting behind it our names, social security numbers, where to have our bags bag sent, and we showed him our IDs.

He took my bag and put some sort of tag on it. This was the last I saw of my stuff. Finally, he handed me a plastic bag with two pairs of navy sweatpants, two T-shirts, and two sweatshirts and directed me to a classroom.

The only time there was yelling was when somebody talked. For the next three days or so, all we did was walk in formation very quietly from one place to another. Getting physicals, shots, fitted for uniforms, the infamous buzz cut… it was incredibly boring, and since I was not used to sleeping in a room with eighty guys, I was really, really tired. I felt like a cow being herded all around that base. In fact, on occasion somebody would let out a "Moooo" just out of earshot of the company commander. It always made me laugh quietly.

We soon moved into the open bay barracks that would become our home for the next two months. This was a very large room lined on either side with bunk beds, and a metal locker between them. I remember first walking in and seeing a giant quote by John F. Kennedy painted on the wall next to the company commander's office at the end of the room. It read:

I can imagine a no more rewarding career, and any man who may be asked in this century what he did to make his life worthwhile, I think can respond with a good deal of pride and satisfaction: 'I served in the United States Navy.'

-President John F. Kennedy

Somehow, seeing that quote brought me comfort regarding this decision I had made.

As the weeks went on, we slowly started to get to know one another. There were not too many times when we were allowed to just sit around and bullshit, but they did happen, and these became times that I looked forward to.

Our marching started to improve, our made beds slowly started to become uniform works of art. Our folded clothes in our cabinets became identical copies, row after row. Eventually our bathroom and floors would glisten with a polished shine. It was not an individual effort. Everything would be reflected as a team. There would be many times that we all found ourselves being punished with some form of physical exercise because someone forgot, or was just too lazy, to do something. "Attention to detail" became words seared into my memory.

The person who would teach us almost everything was our company commander. She was a short, attractive, black female petty officer second class. She was probably in her late twenties or early thirties, and was a constant professional. She would rarely yell, never cursed, and always spoke in a very firm and matter-of-fact way. She also had a reputation for making the "rain man" cometh—meaning we'd do so much exercise in the barracks that the walls would start to sweat from the perspiration in the air, causing drops to fall from the ceiling. She made it rain twice.

She showed up one day wearing sunglasses. She didn't take them off for three days. For reasons I can't remember, I had to go to her office to request permission to leave the barracks and go to the administration office. I knocked twice on her office door and announced myself, "Seaman Recruit Jones here to see Petty Officer Second Class…" and then her last name.

"Come in, Jones," she replied. As I opened the door I could see unmistakably that she had a black eye. Her sunglasses were on her desk in front of her. In that moment she turned into a human being. Her hand rose to touch her smooth dark skin to feel for her shades. She let out an ever-so-quiet gasp, and I saw a moment of pain in her eyes as she looked directly at me. I could tell by the tears starting to form in her eyes that the black eye wasn't from a proverbial doorknob. Her glasses immediately found their way back into place.

"What do you want, Jones?" she asked very sternly.

"Ummm, requesting permission… um…"

"Spit it out, Jones, I don't have all day, recruit!"

I eventually got my words out in an acceptable military manner, and she dismissed me after having me do twenty-five push-ups.

Other than marching practice, the only time we really spent outdoors was marching from one place to the next. It was northern Illinois, and it was now the beginning of December. It was extremely cold and windy most of that month. I did not mind that most of our work was done inside, because the temperature would fall well below freezing and stay in the single digits.

Everybody got sick. It was a kind of cold, I think, and it would last several weeks. It could have been because of the weather, or it could have been the fact that you had so many people from all over the United States living in one room. I remember seeing the bright green coughed up loogies that lined the banks of snow on the side of the paths where we marched.

We were not the only group of guys going through boot camp. There were many other companies at different stages of the training process. We could always tell the companies that were getting close to graduating because they would march really well, sing cadences, and sport several flags at the front of their formations. Companies earned the flags for many different reasons. I can't remember all of them specifically, because I thought the reasons were kind of stupid at the time. The only flag I specifically remember was a fitness flag, and we were awarded it for winning a bunch of events on games day, which involved a bunch of track and field events.

The day I had long awaited finally arrived. We marched to the indoor pool and sat down in a classroom. A Navy diver walked in and told us he was the dive motivator. He went on to explain that he was the person we had to go through if we wanted to become a diver or a SEAL. He would arrange for us to take the physical fitness test that would get us on the track to those careers. He then asked if any of us wanted to be a diver or a SEAL. I am pretty sure that everyone raised his hand. He smiled amusedly and said that he would leave instructions with our company commander for those interested. We then proceeded to the pool area to jump off of a diving platform, tread water, and then swim a length of the pool.

I was shocked to see how many people were scared to jump off of a high dive, and even more so to see how many people did not know how to swim. "Why did you join the Navy," I thought to myself. "You do realize that boats float on water. It's like joining the Army and not knowing how to walk!"

A few days later, we went to take the SEAL test. It was at four in the morning, and as a result almost my entire company, all of whom had raised their hands earlier to show their interest, chose to sleep in rather than wake up and march outside to a cold pool. Just five of us from my company went. When we arrived there, there were about fifty other recruits waiting. The physical training (PT) test consisted of a swim, a run, pull-ups, sit-ups, and ended with push-ups. It was not a difficult test. The target times were not that hard, and neither was the amount of each exercise we had to do. I remember the most difficult part was the swim, since they had us all swim at once. It was like swimming in a triathlon—nothing but assholes and elbows for the first couple laps. I was the only one in my company who passed, securing myself a golden ticket to Basic Underwater Demolition School, or BUD/S, which was a notoriously difficult six month program. Graduation was required to get on the path to becoming a SEAL. We would end up having to wait until after our A-School before we would be allowed to go.

A-School was the technical training the Navy gave you after boot camp. It would become a sailor's rate, which was his job designation in the Navy. Hardly anyone who went to SEAL training graduated from it. So the Navy, in all of its cleverness, made rates for SEAL candidates that they otherwise had a hard time filling, like personellmen (an administration bitch), cooks, or any another less-than-desirable job. This way, SEAL candidates would have something else to fall back on.

Work week was coming. This was when we would work at different positions around the base. The workdays would be around fifteen to eighteen hours long. We were told this was to simulate the long hours of working on a ship.

The day before work week started, our company commander had us stand at attention at the end of our beds, facing the other recruits on the opposite side of the bay. She read off a sheet outlining our workstations for the following week. Just like any job in the world, some would suck big time, and some would be easy.

We had all heard about the worst one. It was working in the deep sink of the galley. Since the deep sink section of the galley was being remodeled, all the cleaning of the pots and pans was done outside—in the middle of winter—with brushes and a hose. As luck would have it, my last name started with a J, and somehow that was the winning lottery ticket that sent me straight to the deep sink. Yay!

It was a miserable week. It got so cold out there that they would have us rotate every fifteen minutes to go back inside to get warm while the other crew went out to pick up where we left off. The pots, pans, and the damn wind and snow never ended. Always the last to return to the barracks at night, I remember walking by other recruits, long asleep in their warm beds. After the third night of always being the last one in, I walked by each of the bunks and slowly and politely said, "Fuck you." Walking to next bunk, "Fuck you… and fuck you, and you, and definitely fuck you!"

By the time I had reached my bed, the entire company was laughing so loud that a night watchman came in and yelled, "Shut your goddamn mouths!"

I made a friend from another company that week. His last name was Johnson, making him one of the lucky winners too. He had made friends with one of the petty officers that ran the kitchen, and that guy gave him a can of Copenhagen. The petty officer told him not to let anybody see him dip, and to keep the can hidden there in the galley.

Johnson was kind enough to share that can of Copenhagen with me through the week. We would find time to meet in the bathroom to take a dip break and talk about how fucked up it was we were sent to Antarctica to work while other people were painting walls inside. We had even heard about a group that was sent to the graduation auditorium to sweep floors, and the petty officer in charge of them was letting them take naps behind the bleachers.

I liked Johnson. He was going to become a "Nuke," meaning that when he finished boot camp he was entering the Navy's nuclear program. This was a very long and academically challenging school that, once completed, led to working with reactors on ships and submarines. He placed really highly on his ASVAB (the military version of the SAT). I have always admired people who could excel academically.

When work week ended, we piled into the auditorium for a speech from the base commander. There were thousands of recruits all lined up in company formation. His speech was rather unmemorable, except one part; he assured us that they were putting nothing in the eggs that was keeping our dicks soft. It was just our nerves. Everyone laughed, because it was true. However, graduation came closer and our nerves came back to us.

Stall number nine at the very far end of the bathroom became a well-kept secret of our company. If that door was closed, you stayed away from it and let whoever was in their jack off in peace. The phrase, "If the stalls a rockin', don't come a knockin'" was thrown around a couple times.

Christmas morning came and the barracks were lined with beautifully wrapped presents. All of our beds had stockings hanging off the ends, with candy flowing over the brim. The sound of "Jingle Bells" quietly being played over the speaker system softly woke us all up…

Just kidding, that shit didn't happen. What did happen, though, was that on Christmas Eve one of the girls from the female companies came into our barracks after we were all in bed and sang "Amazing Grace." I know it's a really hard song to screw up, but she really did a memorable soulful rendition of it, and it was nice to hear a female voice not yelling at me.

The last week of boot camp was a cakewalk. The majority of it consisted of practicing for the graduation ceremony. Our company commander relaxed our sleeping hours a little bit. We even had a movie night in the graduation hall. The movie was Exit to Eden. I remember it very well because there were a lot of tits and ass in it, and the guys would cheer every time a woman would show her boobs. I can only imagine that there weren't any vacancies in stall number nine that night. I liked the movie for a completely different reason. Dan Aykroyd was in it, and at the time I found him attractive.

The graduation ceremony was done perfectly. The marching band played "Anchors Aweigh," and the companies all marched in perfect unison doing a complete lap around what felt like a coliseum with thousands of cheering people. As each company marched by a tall stage where the commanding officer stood, in perfect timing they would smartly turn their heads towards him and render a salute while marching simultaneously.

After the lap, we marched our way to the center of the complex. I remember standing at attention for hours while we had to listen to so many stupid speeches. My eyes were the only things that moved. They spent most of the time looking at the bleachers that lined the immense auditorium. There were just so many brothers, sisters, parents, friends and relatives of all kinds, proudly looking for a glimpse of their son or daughter. Somewhere in the sea of people were my parents, probably thanking God that I had actually graduated.

It was now time for me to head off to my technical training. Prior to joining the Navy, I had agreed to go through the personellman A-school because it was one of the few rates that would allow you go to BUD/S. The school was about six weeks long and was located in Meridian, Mississippi.

CHAPTER 8

Meridian, Mississippi

I was not very excited about my decision to become a personellman, or PN, for short. There was nothing that interested
me about it all.

Months prior to boot camp I had met the Navy recruiter at
the recruitment office located off Riverside Drive in Austin. I
explained that I wanted to be a Navy SEAL, and he showed me the
cheesiest Navy propaganda video ever. It showed a group of
SEALs coming off of a beach, all dressed in black and wearing
black face paint. They carefully snuck into a bunkered office in the
middle of the day, killing one or two guards along the way. The
"SEALs" then left a "bomb" and went back to a boat on the beach.
The video then cut to a view of the outside of the bunker, which
blew up in a 1980's style superimposed explosion. It was horrible.

After the video I turned and looked at him with a huge
question mark on my face. He said, "I know, I know… it's not a
Spielberg film."

This meeting took place a few months before boot camp,
and the movie Navy SEALs with Charlie Sheen had been out
for a couple years. I had it in my mind that being a SEAL was
like that movie. He explained that I had to have a SEAL source
rate in order to be able to attend BUD/S after A-school. Again,
this meant taking a job that the Navy was having difficulty filling. I chose what I thought would be the lesser of the evils.

Funny thing, the recruiter never really gave a definitive description of what SEALs actually do. He was a smooth talker, though. Recruiters are used car salesmen; they are trained to sell you a lemon and make you think you're buying a Porsche.

I arrived at the base in Meridian, Mississippi, with my military orders in hand. After checking into the school and taking care of all the usual administrative requirements, a young petty officer third class showed me to my room. He handed me a Xeroxed paper with all the specific instructions of where and when I needed to be and my uniform requirements on those specific days.

I only had to share my room with one other guy, which was a relief. After unpacking my stuff, I walked around the base. I could not believe how much this place resembled a college campus. It was the weekend, and people were walking around in civies (civilian clothing). Sweet!

A buddy of mine named Burnzy from my boot camp company showed up the next day, a Sunday. Burnzy was from Tacoma, Washington, and was a phenomenal swimmer who held some sort of a state record; I think it was in the breaststroke. We would end up becoming very good friends. He would also end up going to BUD/S with me, but for some reason he had to get his ticket to BUD/S while we were in A-School.

School started that Monday morning with a 0715 muster in the courtyard of the compound. We all marched over to the classroom, found a seat and got comfortable in front of a computer terminal. An older civilian woman walked into the room, introduced herself, and explained that she would be teaching our typing portion of the class. She told us that we would have to be able to type twenty-eight words per minute by the end of the first two weeks of school or we would get sent to the fleet without a rate. I thought, "What did she just say?"

My typing skills were pretty much non-existent; thinking back, I may have typed one or two papers in high school, but only because I had to. This requirement scared the shit out of me. Those who were sent to the fleet without a job ended up cleaning shitters and chipping paint off the hulls of ships. This would also mean no SEAL training. I thought, "That damn recruiter never said anything about this!"

The next two weeks were excruciating. The computers had a program on them with lessons to follow. Graduating from one lesson meant going on to a slightly more difficult one. Each day would end with a test. Each student would be given a piece of paper that had a forty word paragraph on it and would have a minute to copy as much of it as possible before turning it in to be graded.

Over the next two weeks, the students typed their twenty-eight words and tested out of the class one by one. It was the Thursday of the second week when I finally got my twenty-eight words. I can't tell you the relief I felt. The rest of the four weeks were spent learning how to file specific paperwork, fill out different forms, and record data in an archaic database. I drank amazing amounts of coffee, because for a guy like me... well, this was just not my thing.

I was feeling really good about finishing my typing, and it being a payday Friday, I decided to head into town and have some fun. I had made up my mind to find a gay bar, especially since it had been months since I had had any physical contact at all. However, a couple problems remained—how would I find a gay bar, and how would I get there?

I called a taxi company from a payphone in the courtyard and asked to have a cab waiting for me at a gas station not far from the main gate of the base at a certain time. I did this to allow me the time needed to walk the two miles to get there. My plan was to ask the cab driver to take me to a gay bar without him knowing that I'd come from the base.

It was completely dark outside by the time I got there. Not long after I arrived the cab pulled up. The driver was a heavy-set older black man who looked like he had not showered or washed his clothes in couple of days. He had a plastic gold cross hanging from the rear view mirror. As I looked at the guy and his cross, it quickly dawned on me just how deep in the Bible belt I was. It was definitely time to switch my plan up a little. I asked him, "Do you know of a good bar or club around here?" He nodded and named some bar. I replied, "Sounds good."

My plan was to get him already moving, the meter running, and away from the base before I would change my mind. Five minutes later, I leaned forward in my seat, looked at him through his rear view mirror, and asked, "Hey, you know what? I forgot—my brother actually told me he was going to be at some stupid gay bar around here. You happen to know where he was talking about?"

He looked right back at me through the mirror and rolled his eyes toward his left side mirror and said, "Naa, naa, man… I ain't going anywheres near there!" He then pulled the car over, got on his radio, and spoke to the dispatcher, "I got somebody looking to go to Crossroads."

I sat in the back seat, and was cringing that he'd just announced that to every cab driver and God knows who else in the area.

About a second later the radio squealed, "I'll take it." A moment later the same voice came back over the radio and asked the cab driver to meet him at some exit.

When we arrived I handed the cab driver what was on the meter and then some, thinking to myself that it might somehow buy his silence when the anti-gay militia or base police questioned him about me.

While the "don't ask, don't tell" policy was new in the military, it would eventually be clear that it was a load of crap. I felt this instinctively at the time and took pains to cover my tracks. Service members discovered to be gay often received dishonorable discharges. This is a very serious thing. It follows you the rest of your life. People with them couldn't even work at McDonald's at the time. In many states it is the equivalent of a felony conviction.

History would later show my gut instincts were right. The Navy would end up discharging around 300 people a year under DADT. Combine all the services, and you're looking at well over 13,000 people at a minimum losing their jobs because of that policy. To say the military treated the Lesbian, Bi-sexual, Gay, and Transgender (LBGT) community badly is an understatement. It ruined many patriots' lives, leaving in its wake a petri dish to cultivate the growth of abhorrence.

I opened the very loud, dented door, hopped out, and got into the other cab. The new cabby then drove me out in the middle of nowhere. He pulled onto a dirt road and stopped the car. Not a word was said until we stopped, and I asked, "Where are we?"

While he was pushing a button on the meter he replied, "It's up there," and pointed towards some lights in the distance. I gave him his money, again with a little something extra, and I got out of the cab. When he drove off there was no light except what was coming through the trees up the dirt road.

As I came closer I started to hear the sound of club music. This actually gave me some relief, because I was beginning to think that I was walking towards some kind of a trap created by this medieval town to kill gay people. Getting closer, the music got louder, and so did the sound of people. From the outside, I remember it looking like some kind of barn. I passed by a bunch of cars and a couple of guys talking. Their talking stopped once they noticed me, and they continued to stare until I'd made my way to the front door.

As I walked in, I could not believe my eyes. The place was pretty well packed. The music was thumping, and people were laughing, dancing, and unmistakably having a good time. As I was making my way to the bar, a good-looking guy in fairly good shape jumped up on the bar and faced the crowd. He immediately pulled his pants, and his underwear, down to his ankles. The crowd cheered as he held up his hands, pretending to yawn. This raised his shirt above his crotch and left nothing to the imagination.

I liked this place; even the bars in Austin were not this crazy.

It was not long before I was talking to people and dancing. While I was on the dance floor I looked over to the bar to see and older, huskier guy with dark hair staring at me.

I went over and introduced myself, although for the life of me can't remember his name. I know it was something very common like Bob, Mike, or maybe John. Anyway, we ended up talking for hours. He bought me a bunch of drinks, for which I was thankful. After all, I was not exactly rolling in dough at the lowest rank in the Navy, and there was also the matter of my ridiculous taxi fare. As we talked, I knew this was going to be the guy that would break the drought, and he knew it and wanted it as well.

Around three or four in the morning we left the club and went to his big, silver, extended-cab truck. We drove around for a little bit looking for a place where we could safely take care of business. He found a dirt road just off the main road and we got busy. After the first round we talked for little bit before going back at it. By the time we had finished the sun had not yet broken the sky, but it was starting to get lighter out.

He started the truck and agreed to drop me off at the base. As we were driving back, I told him that I did not have a phone number to give him, but if he gave me his we could meet up one night this week, or maybe again next weekend. He told me that he could not give out his phone number because he was married and that he had children, and explained that he lived two hours away.

It was rather shocking for me to hear that. I remember responding by saying something like, "Okay, no problem," but secretly it was kind of a problem for me. Selfishly, I took it as an insult, because at that age I thought I was God's gift to the gay world. I thought this without any regard for his wife, kids, or his situation. I did not spend much time thinking about it after that; in fact, I took it for what it was—a one-night stand.

I ended up going back to that bar one more time before I left. It turned out to be an uneventful night. Much later in life I would find myself surfing through HBO's on demand channel and came across a documentary about that bar. The whole show made me feel really bad for people who were gay in that area. The locals depicted in it were just as I remembered them.

I was now about two weeks from finishing administrative school, and Burnzy and a couple other guys wanted to go to a club were they had heard a lot of hot local girls hung out. One of the guys who accompanied us actually had a car, so we piled in and drove out there.

It wasn't much of a club; it had a bar, a couple of pool tables, and a small dance floor. By the time it ended up getting moderately crowded I was well on my way to a nice beer buzz. We were playing pool when we heard a fight break out in the front of the club. We all turned and looked; whatever was happening, or had happened, died down rather quickly.

Having to take a piss, I started making my way to the bathroom. It was crowded on this end of the club, so there was a lot of bumping shoulders to get there. One guy in particular was pushing his way out of the bathroom. He shoved me pretty good and I remember saying something along the lines of, "What the fuck, man?" He turned and looked at me for a moment and kept moving. I then noticed he had "SECURITY" written on the back of his shirt, and I thought, "Oh, never mind." I figured he needed to get to the front of the bar due to the commotion moments earlier. I then went in the bathroom.

After relieving myself, I opened the bathroom door and stepped out. The next thing I knew I was on the ground fast and hard. The same security guard from moments earlier was standing over me with a black mag lite in his hand, and my mouth was pouring out blood.

My friends immediately ran over to me. Still very disoriented, they quickly ushered me out of the club and to the car. One of the guys stayed in the club to figure out what had happened. When he came out to the car, I asked him, "Did that fucking guy hit me with a fucking five pound flash light?"

He explained that the bouncer had mistaken me for somebody else. I was wearing a light green sweater (which was now covered in blood), and the guy he was looking for was wearing a green long-sleeve shirt. Common mistake... no big deal.

The cops arrived and asked us what happened. I explained the story to them, as did my friends. The two officers walked over to the bouncer who hit me, who was now working the door outside. It became very apparent that they were all friends. They only spoke to him for about three minutes and there was lots of laughing coming from the three of them.

One of the officers walked back over to me and sarcastically said, "You really should go and get that looked at." He walked back over to his car, waved goodbye to the bouncer, and left.

Once I got to the hospital it became apparent that when he had hit me with the flashlight it made my front tooth pierce my top lip, leaving a nice hole and a loose front tooth. The doctor put rubber gloves on and took a good look at it. He then asked me if I'd had anything to drink that night. I told him that I'd had four beers. He looked at me said, "You're going to need stiches. As far as that tooth goes, try not to mess with it too much. I am not going to be able to numb it for you. I am worried how the alcohol might react with any anesthetic. Are you up for it?"

I reluctantly smiled and said, "Sure, why not?" I lied back on the table as he prepared his stainless steel mobile work station. He situated himself by my head and adjusted the dental light above us. My hands innately gripped the sides on the table.

My teeth gritted together as the curved needle carrying the thread pierced the top of the laceration. For the next hour while I lied on his table, painfully getting my lip sewn back together, I thought about how everyone in this town could go to hell, for all I cared. I had not met a single decent human being that was actually from this town the whole time I was there. Two weeks later, I gave Meridian the bird and headed out to Coronado, California, to start my training.

CHAPTER 9

Coronado, California

On my way to California I stopped in Texas to visit my family for a day or two, and also to buy my very first brand new car. It was a blue 1995 Pontiac Sunfire. It was by no means the fastest thing on the road, but it had a sporty look, with a spoiler on the back. It had power everything, a decent sound system, and CD player. The payments weren't too bad, but throw in the insurance and it did eat up one of my paychecks every month.

I headed out on I-10 west towards El Paso. There was an Army doctor named Mick stationed at Fort Bliss with whom I'd had a casual thing. This was also a good midway point to stop along the way. I figured I would get up early the next day and finish my drive to California.

I checked into a room on Fort Bliss, and gave Mick a call. I had met him a couple years prior while on a trip with a photographer friend of mine. We'd been out that way taking pictures in White Sands, New Mexico, and had stopped in Las Cruces for the night to meet up with some friends of the photographer on our way back to Austin. We all went to a gay bar called the Plantation about thirty minutes away in El Paso, and that was where we met.

We had stayed in touch, and he even came out to visit me in Austin before I joined the Navy. When the time came close for him to head back, we were both sitting on the floor next to a stereo. I was shuffling through my CD collection trying to introduce him to some different kinds of music that I liked. Unexpectedly, he started to cry, and as I turned to face him he leaned into my arms and onto my lap. He never talked about why he was crying. I could feel that he was a very lonely person, and by somehow coming to visit me he had managed to escape from whatever loneliness was waiting for him back in El Paso. He told me once that he was supposed to take over his family's business, but had instead gone to medical school without his family's knowledge or consent. I remember feeling incredibly bad for him, and the place in life he was back then.

Mick came by, and it was really good to see him. He looked great, and a lot happier than the last time I'd seen him. We grabbed some dinner, fooled around, and talked for a couple hours. Mick had to work that night at the hospital, so he had to take off. Before going, he told me he would come by in the morning before I left. The drive was going to be a long one and I had to get there by a certain time. I told him that I would have to leave at six a.m. Well, six a.m. came and went. I tried calling and waited as long as I could. By seven I was on the road.

A few hours into the trip I pulled over to get some gas. I remember a guy at the gas station asking me about my car. He said something about how futuristic it looked and kept staring at it. It made me feel really good. I often think back to that time whenever I see one of those cars on the road now. It's not often I see them, but when I do I start to laugh because they usually look like pieces of crap now, and I wonder why I thought it looked so cool back then. It's funny how something like that can so clearly remind me of the excitement I felt almost twenty years ago, driving through the desert on my way to become a SEAL.

It was late at night when I arrived the Naval Amphibious Base in Coronado. The entire compound was located right along the beach. I checked in on the quarterdeck and was given a key and directions to my room. I got a two-man room on the second floor of the barracks. It was right on the beach, and my bedroom door opened up to the Pacific Ocean. Because it was really dark, all I could see of the ocean was the white foam of the waves breaking in the surf. The breeze and the smell of the air were amazing, and absolutely energizing.

It was 0630 Monday morning when my alarm went off. The room had one of those cheap alarm clocks that you would often see in hotels. The alarm made the most horrible sound. I imagine it's the same kind of sound that a nuclear power plant makes when it starts to melt down. However, it did its job and I was soon up, showered, shaved, and in my dress blues, ready to go check in at the PTRR office.

I am not really sure what PTRR stood for. I think it was Pre-training something. It would end up being about a two-week indoctrination and pre-training course before we actually "classed up." After that, we'd go through the three phases of BUD/S.

There was nothing really difficult about PTRR. It was mostly things like getting issued our new uniforms and learning how to prepare for rooms and gear inspections. We would usually have PT once in the morning and then again in the afternoon. The days were fairly stress-free, and the PTRR instructors were trying to get us motivated and ready for training.

The week ended and I made my way out to Hillcrest in San Diego. Hillcrest had a lot of nice restaurants, coffee shops, trendy stores, and of course was where all the cool gay bars and clubs were located.

I found myself in the nicest coffee shop I had ever seen in my life. I actually felt underdressed in there. The tables were draped with linen, and the occasional tapas accompanied somebody's coffee to their table. The baristas and servers wore bowties with very clean, crisp white shirts. I made my way to the coffee bar, found a seat, and ordered a cup. I looked across the shop and could tell that the majority of the patrons were gay. They were almost all male, very neatly groomed, and all wearing designer clothes. It made me feel like a Neanderthal.

Not far from where I was sitting were two good-looking guys. One was younger than the other, and was a few years older than me. He was in shape and had dark, short hair with a fair, smooth complexion. Usually this is not my type of guy, but he had a look about him that I would describe as cute. His friend was more my usual type, he was an older bear with a very kind face. The younger guy left and it was not long before I found myself talking to his friend, Jon. He was a really interesting guy. I am not sure if it was that night or another night, but we did mess around a couple times. However, at the time I was more interested in his younger friend, Jeff. One night I let that accidentally slip out after a couple of drinks. I will never forget the look he gave me when I opened my stupid mouth and said that. I could tell that I had hurt his feelings. Jon and I remained friends long after that. In fact, we still e-mail each other from time to time.

The first phase of BUD/S would end up being the toughest physically. It consisted of eight weeks of basic conditioning, leading up to "Hell Week," which was around the fifth or sixth week of training. I know that it has changed since I went through it.

Hell Week was a test of physical endurance, mental strength, and teamwork. Many people would quit leading up to it, but that week would see the most attrition. More than two-thirds of a given class would likely quit and "ring the bell" that hung just outside of the first phase office. Anyone who quit would have to ring it three times, then place his helmet (upon which was stenciled the student's last name) on the ground just below the bell. By the end of first phase there would be a long line of helmets lying side by side like tombstones constantly serving as a reminder. A reminder of what it takes to make it.

The never-ending discomfort and pain would be enough for most guys to ring the bell. The days of constantly being marginally hypothermic and never being dry would send a lot of guys back to the regular Navy. There would be less than two hours of sleep for most people during that week. Combined with everything else, this would make any sane person question whether or not it was worth it. For most us, it would be the most challenging test we had ever faced.

After clearing Hell Week and finishing first phase, one moves onto second phase. This was about eight weeks of diving. Finally came third phase, which was nine weeks of land warfare training. Most guys who made it through Hell Week would make it through these phases. For those who didn't, it was usually due to academic issues—Dive Physics in second phase being a good example. In third phase you would lose guys to weapons and demolitions safety violations, or for not being competent with said weapons or safety regulations. Every so often, though, a guy would just up and quit out of the blue for no specific reason.

By day one of first phase we had all moved into barracks right on the compound. The rooms had two bunk beds, so there were four guys to a room. Our class number was 201. It was a Monday morning and we all lined up on the grinder. This was the courtyard located in the middle of all the four-sided buildings where the different phase offices were located. In the front of the grinder was a large wooden stage. On the concrete slab that made up the courtyard were painted frog feet. There was a break in the building on the side that faced the beach. Between the grinder and the beach was our building, with all our rooms in it. There was no walking allowed on the grinder—come to think of it, I don't recall much walking being allowed at all. Our class consisted of about 140 guys. All of us lined up on the courtyard facing the stage.

An instructor walked out of the adjacent first phase office and walked onto the stage. Our class leader yelled, "Instructor Hurley!"

Then the entire class yelled out, "Hooyah, Instructor Hurley!" "Hooyah" would become synonymous with many things, including "yes," "yes, sir," "I will do it," and as a sign of motivation.

Instructor Hurley was our class proctor. It was his job to try and keep as many students motivated as possible to finish that phase. It was every other instructor's job to make you quit. Instructor Hurley was a horrible proctor. In fact, he was no better than the rest of the instructors, and on some occasions was much worse.

The day started with the command "Hit the surf!" That was the command for everyone to run as fast as they could to the ocean and get completely wet and then run as fast as possible back to his spot on the grinder. I remember that morning temporarily wearing a freshly pressed and starched uniform.

The instructors were like sharks! They would actively look for the weak and single them out. Those who failed to keep up with what the instructor was doing on the stage were torn apart. There were about five other instructors constantly looking for those who could not keep up. When they found one they would make him run to the beach or do a more demanding physical exercise. This went on for about two hours before they had us run out to the beach for a conditioning run.

Everyone stood in formation on the beach, wet and exhausted. Then big white trucks with off-road tires pulled up. A loudspeaker announced, "Everyone get wet and sandy! HURRY THE FUCK UP!" Everyone immediately ran into the surf, got wet, ran back, and rolled around in the powdery beach until we were all completely covered in sand.

By the time we'd returned in formation, an instructor was standing on the beach in his combat boots, shorts, and a blue instructor T-shirt. The rest of us were wearing our issued olive drab Army greens and what used to be our black polished combat boots. The instructor very quickly started to run south on the soft sand of the beach. We all followed him in pursuit while maintaining formation.

It did not take long for the pack to slowly get longer and longer. Faster runners passed the slower runners and soon the formation was almost a quarter mile long. The instructors followed in their trucks, harassing the slower runners over their PA system. Before long, I found myself being separated from the pack. I would try to sprint back up, but eventually they were just too far ahead of me.

By this time there was a second instructor leading a pack of guys who could not keep up. I looked back and saw him a hundred yards behind me. If he caught up, I would be in the goon squad. This meant that after the guys who'd been able to keep up with the lead instructor finished their run, whoever was left would remain at the finish line doing sprints, bear crawling, or whatever else the instructors felt like ordering. The instructors would occasionally have the goon squad do some kind of race, and would release the winner to join the rest of the class.

Needless to say, the second instructor caught up to me. By the time the conditioning run was finished, only twenty guys had been able to keep up with the instructor for the whole five or six miles. We were gooned for about thirty minutes and then released to run to the chow hall for lunch.

As we jogged to the chow hall, my feet loved the fact that they were on solid ground. Running on soft sand was incredibly difficult, especially with wet combat boots. I remember trying to follow the footsteps of somebody ahead of me. It did not seem to work out that well. Eventually, I would learn the best way for me personally to run on that kind of surface was to go as flatfooted as possible and, for some reason, to try not to look down while running.

A highway ran down the center strand, separating the base. The other side of the base faced the bay. It was on that side that the chow hall was located, about a mile away from the compound. We would have to jog in formation every time we went to and from chow.

When we arrived at the chow hall, we did not have much time. I think we actually only had about twenty minutes to get our food, eat, and then head back for log PT. I ate my lunch quickly, and sat in the chair watching everybody else finish. I was exhausted! That morning had been a real shock to me. I had always thought that I was in good shape, but apparently I was nowhere near the condition in which I needed to be. I was strong; I had lifted weights as far back as fourteen years old. But this was different. I needed endurance as well as strength— much more endurance than I'd thought.

Not long after that, we found ourselves back on the beach. We were separated into boat crews. A boat crew usually consisted of seven guys of around the same height, one of whom would be appointed the crew leader. This was almost always the senior ranking guy of the group. The smallest group of guys was called the smurf crew. I ended up somewhere in the middle.

Before the instructor arrived, we had all grabbed a log (think telephone pole) and placed it in front of our boat crew. We all stood at attention awaiting the instructor's arrival. When he arrived our class leader gave out the customary "Instructor Washington" And we all yelled out, "Hooyah, Instructor Washington!"

The instructor began the log PT by ordering us to the surf. The log PT commenced with our boat crew all having to simultaneously lift the log above our heads and hold it there. We would hold it for so long that it would start to drop towards our heads. If anyone let it fall down below his head, that would bring in the sharks who were waiting patiently for any student who was not putting out.

After this, the instructor would give the command for us to position the log across our chest, sit down, and start doing sit ups with it. Then we were instructed to get up with it and run it up and over the twenty-foot sand berm that separated us from the ocean. There would be all sorts of other exercises and races we would do with those logs. We were at the mercy of the instructors' imaginations.

For the crew that was having the most trouble was reserved "Old Misery." This log looked like a damn sequoia. It was so thick that you could not wrap your arms around it, making it very difficult to maneuver. Additionally, it was heavy as hell! I found myself under that log many times over the next few weeks.

After an hour or two, the instructors decided that log PT was not to their liking. The whole class found themselves locking arms in the surf zone, lying down in the water. This was known as surf torture, and I hated it more than anything. It was a way of making you really cold, really quickly. Nothing makes time come to a screeching halt like being cold. The Pacific waters were far from tropical, and before long we would find ourselves shivering uncontrollably. As our bodies started to become hypothermic, the instructors would have us get out and run up and down the berm a few times to get our body temperatures back up. Then back in the drink we went.

As I lay there, I would try to think of things that would distract me from being so cold. I would imagine hanging out at a nice warm bar with friends, or looking for clouds and figuring out what they resembled. Though I would try these tricks many times, nothing ever really worked. I was always there and in the moment.

That day surf torture would last all the way to dinner. As we jogged to the chow hall, the class was visibly crushed. Our class leader started a cadence, and it did a good job of improving morale on our way. The day was done after dinner, and I think we lost three guys that day. The attrition would continue at a rate of two to three guys every day until Hell Week.

The rest of the week would be similar to the first day, the difference being that the evolutions, or types, of physical training would change. There would be four-mile timed runs that we had to pass, two-mile ocean swims, an obstacle course, lap swimming, drown-proofing, and underwater knot tying, just to name a few of the challenges we faced.

The weekend came, and I remember how sore and beaten I felt. Some of the guys met up at clubs and bars downtown. I went to bed early and slept until 11 a.m. the next day. Saturdays were the only real day off. Sundays were spent cleaning rooms and getting everything ready for the inspections that came early Monday morning. These were extremely difficult to pass. The tiniest bit of sand in the corner could cause mean failure. If our knives were not sharp enough, or our uniforms were not crisp, or the slightest smudge on our belt buckles was discovered, we found ourselves very quickly wet and sandy, and our rooms completely destroyed. It was not uncommon to spend the entire day Sunday preparing our rooms and gear for these inspections.

As the weeks went on, I remember getting really good at them. Our rooms, gear, and uniforms became perfection. There came a point before Hell Week that the instructors would sneak sand in their pockets and place it in our rooms prior to an inspection. Instructors would run out of ways to fail a guy, so they would just make shit up. "Jones, your fucking face is annoying! You fail! Hit the surf!" or "You had a professional polish those boots! That's a fail, cheater! Hit the surf!" Every once in awhile a group would pass an inspection, allowing them to relax while everyone else got the beat down.

I remember one group that had passed the inspection and were told to stand outside near the entrance to the beach. We all ran by them one by one as the instructors made their way to each room, sending guys to the surf. While some guys were waiting for an instructor who was late getting to the inspection, another instructor asked them what the hell they were doing just standing there. Before they could respond, the instructor yelled, "Hit the surf!"

Eventually, we all figured out that no matter how clean our shit was, we were more than likely going to fail. However, not cleaning our rooms was ten times worse than failing with all our gear, room, and uniforms squared away.

One of the days leading up to Hell Week we all found ourselves at the pool. This was an Olympic-size swimming pool. Before entering the pool we would have to go through what they called "de-con." This was a series of water jets that surrounded a group of about thirty guys at a time and sprayed freezing cold water on them. Everyone had to stay in this until the instructors deemed them clean enough to enter the pool area.

Thinking that today was going to be just another time at the pool, I was pretty excited. I had no problems with swimming laps or with the drown-proofing exercises. Drown-proofing involves binding the hands and feet, then being thrown into the deep end of the pool. We would have to sink to the bottom, push ourselves up get a breath of air, and then immediately let it out so that we could sink to the bottom again. I actually found this exercise to be really relaxing.

But this day was going to be much different; this day was going to be the beehive. The instructors had us all fill our masks up with water and do flutter kicks on the side of the pool to start. This was not very difficult for me since I was able to easily breathe out of my mouth. Some guys had trouble with it initially, but quickly learned how to keep the water from running down their noses and into their lungs. It was kind of funny to hear guys struggling with it; it would sound like they were drowning.

After we finished, the instructors had all the one hundred-plus guys stand up and they checked to ensure that our masks were still full of water. They instructed us to get in the deep end. Slowly, as we were all treading water, they had us gather closer together. The instructors were also in the pool at this point, slowly pushing us closer and closer together. As this was happening I thought that this was easy. I couldn't see much, but it was not that difficult.

It was not long before it became extremely crowded and hard to tread water. Then I heard it—the unmistakable sound of somebody panicking near the center of the mass, close to where I was. What happened next was like a scene out of World War Z. One panicking person turned in to two, two into four, four into eight, and so on. Meanwhile, the instructors were tirelessly pushing the students closer. It became mass panic!

People were climbing over other people, pushing them under so they could get air. Trying to keep my wits, I dove under the mass. Looking up it reminded me of an anthill after someone stepping on it. I searched desperately for a light to shine through opening. I found one! Immediately I broke to the surface and took a huge breath before being pushed down again. It was not enough! Panic started to come over me. Then an idea hit me, I would swim under the mass to the outside of the circle. At least that way I would not have 360° of mass-panicking people around me, holding me under the water.

As I swam toward the edge, the unmistakable outline of an instructor in his wetsuit met me under the water and gave me a wave off, signaling he was not going to let me swim to the edge. I immediately fought my way back into the middle of the mass, completely panicking now. I was somehow able to get two good breaths. As I was pushed under, I could see the instructors swimming to a body that was slowly drifting to the bottom. Again, I fought to get some air, only this time I was not able to fight my way through. I started swimming to the side about two feet under the kicking legs and was met by another instructor. I gave him the international sign for I am about to die, waving my hand across my throat. He returned the gesture with an exaggerated shrug, as if to say, "I don't give a shit." Somehow, I made it up for air, and shortly thereafter they secured the beehive.

Holy crap, that was such a horrific nightmare! I remember seeing blood in a few of the water-filled masks because guys had gotten kicked, elbowed, or whatever. Guys who had passed out were on side of the pool, hooked up to oxygen. I remember leaving the pool feeling like a gorilla had just raped me.

"Thank God that is over," I thought, "...or is it?"

I asked one of the guys if we were going to have to do that again. I remember his response, "I really, really hope not."

It turned out that we did not have to do it again.

Hell Week was now just a week away, and it was a Friday. I was feeling pretty down because I was failing a lot of the timed events. You would have to pass at least half of these to move on to the second phase. My nemesis was the timed run. I was never a very good runner growing up. Burnzy came over and gave me the "don't sweat it" speech, and said that a bunch of guys were going out to grab some dinner. A group of about fifteen of us had dinner at an Italian restaurant in Coronado.

After that I drove to a gay bar called Flicks in Hillcrest. It was there I ran into Jon and Jeff, who were with a group of friends. We hung out for a few hours, knocking back drinks. Jeff and I left the bar together and went to his place. We ended up spending the night together. The next morning I could tell that Jeff thought it was a mistake. It bothered me that he felt that way because, like I said earlier, I thought I was something special.

Jeff was timid in the morning and ushered me to the door. I walked to my car and sat down in the driver's seat, wondering what the hell I'd done. I started the car and was about to back out when Jeff came outside for a jog. I put the car in park, and ran up to ask him if we could talk for a second. It was obvious that I had scared him, which surprised me because I could have sworn he'd seen me. He explained that he needed to go run before he went to work, driving home the point that it was time for me to leave. I nodded my head and said, "Okay, I'm sorry I scared you." Then I walked back to my car and drove away.

The gay community in San Diego was all about how much money you had, the clothes you wore, the friends you had. At the time, Jeff was an officer in the Navy and had lots of rich friends like Jon. I was almost the lowest rank in the Navy. I did not have much money, and whenever I bought clothes it took an act of Congress. By the time I had driven back to the base I had convinced myself that was the reason. I would later find out the real reason was that he was already seeing somebody.

A couple years later, I was watching TV and saw that a coward by the name of Andrew Cunanan had murdered him. Cunanan was the man who also later murdered Gianni Versace. It was crushing to hear that. I had often thought about Jeff, and would wonder when our paths would cross again. Realizing that was never going to happen brought on disbelief, followed by shocking emptiness. I can only imagine what his family went through.

The next week came and went. It was Sunday night, and I remember being very nervous. Hell Week would start with a thing called, "Break Out." It would be the only fun part of Hell Week. We were all (not really) sleeping in the barracks, twenty-five yards from the grinder. We were not allowed to wear watches, but I think it was sometime around 10 p.m. when a loud explosion went off in the hallways. "Here we go," I thought to myself.

Machine guns started firing, and concussion grenades were exploding all over the place. We heard our class leader yell, "Muster on the grinder!"

We all ran there only to be met with fire hoses and then smoke grenades.

"Get a boat crew, muster!" the class leader yelled.

We all scurried in the chaos to try and find our boat crews in the smoke and noise. Our crew leaders ran up to report that we were all up. The instructors then ordered us back to the beach. A whistle signaled us to hit the deck.

BOOM! Another concussion grenade exploded, really close to me that time. A high-pitch ringing was in my ear as we all low-crawled to the beach. "Hit the surf!" an instructor announced over a megaphone.

We all got up and ran to the surf.

"On your bellies" he yelled again.

We crawled our way as fast as possible to the surf and, just like that, the "break out" was over. We then were instructed to link arms and start the surf torture. It went on and on for hours.

At some point around two or three in the morning I let go of the two guys I was linked to and started walking towards the instructors. The class started yelling "Don't do it, Jones. Don't do it!" I walked up to the master chief, shivering uncontrollably, and told him, "I'm done." I was the first one to quit in Hell Week.

That was definitely not my proudest moment. I don't think it actually hit me until I realized that I was going to have to tell my family. The only person that I know who has been through anything remotely close to this was my dad. I walked to the payphone and remember very well dropping those quarters, and then hearing the sound they made, and then hearing the dial tone awaken on the receiver. Every digit I pushed made an almost deafening tone.

The phone started to ring; it was late, so it must have rung four or five times.

My dad picked up his end of the line and spoke in a tired voice, "Jones residence."

I started to hang the phone up, but stopped and put it back up to my ear. "Dad…" I said very quietly.

"Oh no, Brett. I am really sorry," he said softly before I could even tell him what happened.

I just stood there and started to cry.

CHAPTER 10

Keflavik, Iceland

My last couple weeks in California were spent on the phone with my detailer. This was the person who would ultimately decide my fate after quitting training. As luck would have it, he was not sending me to a ship to work as an admin. The Navy needed military police officers, and they thought a good place to recruit them was from the SEAL dropouts.

This meant going to San Antonio, Texas, to receive the appropriate training, then flying out to Keflavik, Iceland. The whole thing sounded pretty good—minus the Iceland part. I tried to negotiate with the detailer for something a little more tropical, perhaps. But he insisted that it was a good place and that people liked it there. Honestly, I had no choice. Detailers had a difficult job, and I respected that. Burnzy dropped out a day later and would end up out there with me as well. It brought some comfort knowing that I would have at least one friend there.

I flew out on a military chartered plane. It was an incredibly bumpy ride. Looking out the window, I could see the shoreline as we started to descend. The Keflavik NATO base was on the very southeastern tip of the island. The water looked very clear, especially close to the rocky shores. The terrain was very rugged, but surprisingly green. Not much in the way of trees, but it looked really interesting to me. The architecture looked very boxy and block-like. The homes and buildings did not have much personality to them, especially on the base.

As I got off the plane, I was greeted by the petty officer who was to be my sponsor. A sponsor is appointed to help with a smooth transition to a new base. He was there to help me get checked in, show me around the base, and let me know about the policies and procedures of the base and the command. He was a nice guy, and after he helped get me into my room, I told him, "Hey, man. I know it is your day off and you would probably rather spend it with your family instead of showing me around all day. If I have any questions, I will just ask somebody."

"Thanks a lot, Jones. Here is my number. If you need anything just call," he said, and handed me a folded piece of paper. Then he reached to shake my hand and said, "Welcome aboard, Jones."

I returned his smile and gave him a sincere, "Thank you."

This would be home for almost two years.

We lived in a barracks-style building. Everyone who worked in base security and was single or unaccompanied by their families lived on the first floor and shared a room with somebody. Those who were a petty officer or above had their own room. Burnzy and I would end up sharing a room. Everyone shared a large bathroom located in the middle of the building.

My first day on the job was spent sitting in the chief's office, listening to him go over all the requirements that I would need to accomplish before they would issue me a badge and allow me to hit the road on my own. There were actually a lot of requirements; they obviously took their jobs seriously.

While I spent the days trying very hard to become qualified, I often spent my time alone thinking about what had happened in SEAL training. It would haunt me every night for a long time to come. I would hear stories from guys that arrived later, telling me about people that I knew that had gone on to graduate. Somehow, hearing these stories made me feel even more depressed.

There were about six to ten of us at any given time who had quit SEAL training. I quickly discovered the easiest way for me to deal with the depression of failing was alcohol. We all dealt with it that way.

Our work rotation was two twelve-hour shifts, back-to-back, followed by two days off. After two cycles of that you would do a three-day shift with two days off. It was like having two weekends every week. The base had two enlisted bars, and they had just finished dropping two million on renovating one of them. The alcohol on base was significantly cheaper than out in town, so we found ourselves spending most of our time there. If we were working the midnight shift we would go to the barracks and hang out in each other's rooms after the shift and drink. Nine times out of ten, the conversation would slowly migrate back to training or SEALs as we got drunker. Guys would tell funny stories of things that happened to them, or tell war stories of how miserable something was for them... it just went on and on.

A very peculiar thing developed, or had already developed before I got there. Guys would judge you based on how long you made it in training; even guys who had never gone to BUD/S. Those who had made it the furthest in Hell Week had the best credentials. Those who made it to at least Hell Week had decent standing. But if you quit in the first couple weeks, you found yourself sitting on the sidelines of the conversation. It became a taboo subject to talk about ever going back, because nobody ever did. Those who brought it up would almost get shunned, in a way. It was a very negative culture.

The Icelandic people as a whole were very attractive, especially their women. Almost all of the women had beautiful porcelain skin, and light brown or blonde hair. They would somehow keep their figure and beauty even as they got older. Whenever we would make the forty-minute drive to Reykjavík to go to the clubs, I always felt underdressed. They took a lot of pride in their appearance and clothing. Everything was really expensive in Iceland. At the time, I judged everything off of the price of a beer, which cost around eight dollars a pint.

The day came when I received my badge and was out rolling the streets of the base on my own. I started on the night shift, and other than weekend nights it was a long, slow shift. There were two gates that had to be manned during the day, and only the main gate had to be manned at night. We would rotate the gate duty, because it was horribly boring. You would spend hours sitting in a guard shack with nothing but your thoughts, every once in awhile getting out to either salute an officer's car or wave in an enlisted person's. Sometimes hours would go by between cars at night. I found myself an old notebook and started writing poems to help pass the time. I came across that book just a year ago while going through some old boxes. As I read them, I realized just how lonely, and depressed, I was out there.

Iceland can be a strange place. During the winter the nights become incredibly long. In fact, the sun only comes up for a little while. It rises above the surrounding mountains, trails across those distant peaks, and then dives back down. The summers are the exact opposite. I remember coming out of bars at three in the morning and it being bright out. It was now October, and the weather was dropping below freezing at night.

One night around 2230 hours, a very pregnant black female officer and I were out riding around in a marked Jeep Cherokee, checking doors to ensure they were locked, when we got a call over the radio. The dispatcher announced that this would be a training exercise only. The training staff of the security department would do these from time to time to keep people fresh and fight complacency. We were to investigate a domestic disturbance out at a remote site, and she instructed our unit and one other to respond.

We were sent to an old abandoned giant microwave satellite dish about five miles away, across a huge field of volcanic rock and located just meters from the rocky shore. We had been there many times. A lot of us would go out there and climb the ladder of the five-story satellite dish to see the view from the top. It was spectacular, even at night—especially when the ocean was turbulent.

As we made our way down the dark paved road that led to the site, I looked at my partner's belly and said, "They do know you're pregnant, right?"

I could tell she gave it some thought, and then the radio squealed, "Training exercise only, training exercise only. We received a report of shots fired."

She turned on our lights and started to speed up. The other unit was about fifty yards behind us on the long, straight road. They called out to us, coming over kind of broken, "Watch out for black guys!"

With the radio in my hand I turned and looked at my partner. I said, "Did they just say, 'Look out for black guys?' What the hell does that mean?" I could tell it bewildered her too.

Moments later we came up to what looked like a little rainwater on the road. Traveling at about fifty miles per hour, we hit the patch of black ice the other unit had just tried to warn us of.

The car turned in place while still hurling forward. A second later we were facing the unit that was following us. The vehicle kept spinning, somehow staying in the same lane, almost pointing us back forward again.

For a moment I thought that by some act of God we were going to make it out of this.

Before we'd fully reached that forward-facing direction, we hit the dry road. The tires gripped it, causing the Jeep to flip.

My side was the first to hit the road. Very clearly I remember my window shattering and all the tiny pieces of glass flying up towards the driver, then dropping back down and out the window as the car continued to roll.

As the car rolled onto its roof, the ceiling caved about six inches and hit my head pretty hard. I felt us drop a little, and we continued to roll for what seemed like forever, until we came to a jolting stop.

Confused and dazed, I heard the radio, still working, going crazy with traffic from the unit behind us, "Dispatch, dispatch! We just had a major vehicle accident involving unit three! Send an ambulance and a fire truck. There is gas pouring everywhere!"

The driver's side of the car was on the ground. I was hanging in my seatbelt above my partner. I looked at her and asked, "Are you okay?"

She did not respond.

I was trying to find a way out while fighting to free myself from the seatbelt. The metal of the car was so crushed in that the only exit I could see was a small crawlspace through the back. Somehow I was able to push the release button on the seatbelt, and I immediately fell towards my partner. While I dropped on her I was careful not to touch her anywhere near her stomach.

I felt her move and she made a moaning sound. As I made my way through the twisted metal to the back I could start to see what had caused that falling feeling. We had somehow rolled off the road, which had been built up about ten feet above the jagged lava field. I could see the other officers trying to negotiate the terrain to get to us.

They were about halfway between the road and me when, free of the wreckage, I stood up and said, "Help me get her out, I think she's hurt." I said this thinking the car was going to explode from the gas leak.

Suddenly, I felt sweat dripping down my face, I wiped it and quickly realized that it was blood. Just then my head really started hurting. I felt myself losing consciousness. I grabbed onto the back of the car and tried to breathe. It felt like a head rush.

The other officers were now with me, and I said, "I think the only way to get to her is through here," and I pointed to the small tunnel from which I'd just crawled. One of them crawled in while the other communicated with the emergency responders on the radio. I let go of the truck for a second to get a better view of what he was doing and I immediately passed out.

I woke up moments later on the ground with the officer telling me not to move. Everything had a fog around it, like when you spend too much time in a pool with your eyes open underwater. It took a good bit of time for the paramedics to load me up in a stretcher and get me back up to the road. Meanwhile, all other available hands worked on getting her out. Before the paramedics loaded me into the ambulance, I pulled the oxygen mask from my face and asked a paramedic if she was okay. He responded, "I think she is going to be fine."

The night was filled with x-rays, all kinds of brain tests, and them removing glass from the inside of my ears. I had various cuts and bruises all over my body, but was for the most part a very lucky guy. My partner, by an act of God, was in better shape than me. She suffered mainly from shock, and her baby was perfectly healthy and still inside her. We both were released by the next night.

The base commander had put the mangled marked car on the main road with a sign that said, "Drive Carefully." Although I know he had the best intentions, I still thought it was kind of a dick move. He should have at least had the light bar and graphics taken off the car first.

The doctor put me on light/limited duty for a week after that, which meant my whole shift was spent at the guard shack at the main gate.

We worked with the Icelandic Police when we were at the gate. They had a very similar shift to ours. We would patrol the inside of the base and they would patrol the town of Keflavik just outside it. One of us would man the gate, and one of them would man it with us. We would monitor incoming traffic, and they would monitor outgoing traffic. We all got to know each other really well. Every so often we would team up to do a joint patrol on the base. Either they would ride in our car or we would ride in theirs.

There was one officer with whom I really enjoyed working. He was approaching seventy and looked every bit of it. He was about six feet tall and very skinny. The guy acted like he was twenty years old. He was extremely energetic, he always talked about his sexual conquests with local women, and he cursed worse than any sailor I knew. He would go on for hours about how the Icelandic air and diet made him so youthful. He would often end one these rants by smacking his chest and proclaiming himself a Viking.

Not long after the accident, I went down to the gate to relieve the pregnant officer. My Icelandic Viking buddy showed up shortly after that. He came in and greeted me, "Great fucking day, eh Jonesy!"

He took off his jacket and hung it on the wall. He sat down in his chair in front of the window facing outgoing traffic and pulled something out of his lunch bag and started eating it. I had been looking at his reflection through my window as he walked in, and I turned and looked at him. He had a large chunk of something white and frozen and he was using his pocketknife to shave pieces off and eat it. I asked him what it was.

He turned from his window and replied, "Good fucking Viking shit, man"

"What is it, though?" I asked again.

"Fucking shark, man," he replied, turning back to his window.

"What does it taste like?" I asked.

"Like fucking shark," he said condescendingly.

I started laughing and said, "Uh, okay."

He turned back around and said, "Try some shit, man." Then he handed me what looked like an ice cream sandwich minus the cookie bread, with wax paper wrapped around the bottom half. I reached over and grabbed the bar of shark from him, careful to keep my hand on the paper part. I studied it carefully while pulling my knife out of my pocket. It actually looked like vanilla ice-cream. I put it up to my nose to see if I could smell anything, and to my surprise… absolutely nothing. I shaved a piece of it off, held it on the end of my knife, and handed him his lunch back.

I put the knife up to my mouth and carefully pulled the meat off with my teeth. I let it sit in my mouth for a second and couldn't taste anything. I started to chew, which sped up the thawing process, and all hell broke loose in my mouth. It tasted like every fish in the world had died and rotted in my mouth instantaneously. It was so bad that it immediately permeated my nostrils. It was like dead-fish-flavored wasabi. I immediately spit it on the ground inside the shack and stepped outside to finish spitting it out of my mouth, while he remained inside laughing.

Another officer pulled up and parked his car to deliver my lunch. He stepped inside and straightaway asked if the pregnant officer's water had broken in there. I told him, "No… that is the smell of his nasty-ass lunch!" pointing toward him eating away at the fish. He just smiled, showing what remained of his teeth. It took hours for that flavor and odor to leave.

As Christmas approached, I was finding myself at a new low. As far as the Navy was concerned, I was doing great. I had received a promotion, and was doing really well at work. My reports needed very little correcting, and I was proactive in doing my part to help the team. But it felt like my life was going nowhere, and the loneliness was just overwhelming. I was almost twenty-two, and just wanted to be able to go out on a date. Being gay at the time was incredibly difficult. There was just nobody to talk to. Occasionally, I would call up old friends on the phone, but it would be very rare because it was so expensive. Sometimes I would get letters from them, and that was always nice.

One night, I went to downtown Reykjavík with a couple of guys, including Burnzy, to check out the clubs. It was always the same thing. We would drink a lot, and think we were the coolest things ever.

This night I got into a fight with a guy for looking at me wrong. On the way back to the car, in a drunken stupor, I had punched him in front of his girlfriend. He fell to the ground, not hurt too badly, thank God. Burnzy quickly sprang into action, pulled me off the guy, and threw me into the car. The guy's girlfriend immediately went to his aid, and then came running after me in tears. I remember the ride back to the base, and how one of the guys thought it was so funny. He thought Burnzy should not have jumped in. On the ride home Burnzy pulled the car over and got into it with the guy.

All I thought about was their faces looking at me, and how I was slowly becoming someone I hated. Later in life, Burnzy would tell me that when we got back to the barracks I told him how I regretted what I had done, and how bad it made me feel.

Around this time Burnzy was dating a beautiful Icelandic girl. In fact, she was probably the prettiest girl I had seen in Iceland. She was amazing to look at. Things were getting really serious between the two of them, and we would often all hang out, especially since we shared a room.

He loved to surf. It is what he dreamed of doing constantly. I remember us going out with an older couple that was stationed on the base together. They let us use their wet suits and surfboards, and we all drove out to a black-sanded beach not far from the base. It was freaking freezing, but it was also fun just to do something other than drink and smoke (Oh yeah... I'd picked up smoking). He was a very relaxed and care-free person.

Christmas came and went, and finally one day I told him and his girlfriend that I was gay. He did not believe it at first, but was very accepting about it and really seemed to understand how miserable it was for me in Iceland. It was not long after that that he was out-processed from the Navy. It absolutely killed me that he was leaving. I had no idea who I was going to talk to after that. I never saw him again, but we would talk on the phone from time to time for a year or so. About fifteen years later, Facebook magically happened, and we have stayed in touch that way. He was a good friend.

Sometime around my birthday in February, we all went to the bar on base. We stayed for hours, drinking, playing pool, and throwing darts. The bar closed and we headed over to the Mar-Bar. The Marines had a bar in their building, which was right next to ours, and would often have after-hour parties. As we staggered over there, we saw one of the most amazing things ever.

The Northern Lights were in full effect. I had seen them a couple times during the winter, but it wasn't like this. This night was a different story altogether. They stretched all the way across the entire sky. They looked like giant green glowing curtains above us. It reminded me of the awe and breathtaking beauty of seeing my sister standing on the edge of the Grand Canyon for the first time. Drunk or not, it was an incredible sight.

I was now on the day shift and was out patrolling the neighborhoods on the base early in the morning. It was still cold and dark outside. The dispatcher came over the radio and told me that the Icelandic Fire Department had called to report a suicide at one of the large airplane hangars located near the flight line.

I pulled my patrol truck up to the giant hangar, got out, and walked through a four-foot break between the large front hangar doors that stretched almost five stories high. I saw a senior military police officer talking to one of the firemen next to a four-story building located inside the hanger. I walked over to him, and he told me that the crime scene was at the top of that building. He then instructed me to ensure it was secured because the Naval Criminal Investigative Service (NCIS) was on its way.

I climbed up the stairwell that led to the roof of the building, which was about twelve feet from the ceiling of the hangar. As I got closer, I could hear a group of guys talking in Icelandic. I soon saw a man lying on the ground next to a five-foot high tool cabinet. He was in his camouflage uniform with a rope around his neck, which had been cut from an I-beam that ran across the hangar ceiling. I immediately turned to the group of firemen and instructed them very sternly to leave. They left and I taped off the crime scene around his body, making sure not to look at him.

Moments after I'd finished, the senior officer came up to the roof and said, "Can you believe those fucking fireman, fucking up the scene like that?"

"I can believe it." I replied.

Looking down at the body he said laughing, "That motherfucker is dead as hell!" We both shared a laugh because it made everything a little less awkward. He turned towards the stairwell and said, "I am going to go down and wait for the NCIS. Stay here and make sure nobody comes up."

The area on the roof was not that big. Alone in that small area, I found myself closer to the body than I felt comfortable with. Up to this point I had made sure not to look too closely at it, but as time went by I found myself getting more curious. I told myself, "It's just a dead body. It's no big deal, Brett."

The first things that I noticed were his eyes. They were shockingly blue, yet very lifeless. His face was young; he had to have been only in his mid- to late twenties. The next thing I noticed was that his neck was obviously broken. You could see what looked like his neck bones protruding out the top, where the rope had once been on the left side of his neck. His body was flat on the ground, with the exception of one leg which was slightly bent off the ground at the knee. I saw a picture of what looked like his family on the ground, not far from his body.

As I looked at his empty stare, my mind drifted back to the hotel room my brother had dropped me off at after my parents had kicked me out of the house. I remembered feeling so worthless and lonely that night. I also remembered the existential debate I'd had in my mind, followed by the fierce pitting of my greater self against the lesser, darker, yet oddly comforting, presence. As I looked at this man, all I could think about was how lucky I was to have had the strength to fight through it and somehow find my worth, even though it seemed like the entire world hated me and people like me.

I later heard that the reason that the guy hung himself was because he was having an affair, and apparently could not live with the guilt.

A new guy had just arrived who had failed out of BUD/S. His name was John, and he was a tall, blonde, muscular guy. He was a very attractive person. He had not been there long when he was sent to guard an ammunitions bunker that was having some alarm issues.

While he was sitting in the guard shack next to the bunker, he pulled his gun out and shot himself in the leg on purpose. He called out over the radio that he had been shot, which sent everyone into frenzy. He would later explain that he did it because he wanted to see what it felt like.

I knew the real reason he did it, though. He did it because he had failed himself, just like the rest of us had. It was an escape from having to deal with the shame and guilt he felt from not accomplishing the dream that we all had shared at some point.

The drinking and partying did not end. The weather was getting warmer, and something had to change. If I was never going to be a SEAL, I needed to accept that and move on! If I was going to be a SEAL, then I needed get that damn fire burning and get back to work! This person who was content to live in gray mediocrity with a beer in one hand and a cigarette in the other seriously had to go.

Fortunately, I found a path forward. Dennis was a born-again Christian who attended church regularly. He was the golden child of the department, and he was a really nice guy. He had also quit BUD/S, but had managed not to get sucked into the same trap of guilt and depression as me and the other SEAL dropouts, largely because he lived his Christian values. He was a positive influence, and I was going to do what I could to become friends with him.

It was not long before we were going to church together, working out together, and becoming really good friends. Dennis was an amazing athlete. He was one of those guys to whom God had given what I call the "freak gene." No matter what or how much that guy ate, he was always in freakishly good shape.

I actually enjoyed going to church. I did not always agree with what was being talked about, but ninety-five percent of the time it offered good, solid teachings and advice about how to live life like a man—not like the selfish child I was becoming.

Dennis was a great influence on me, and I will never forget the kindness he showed me. Not long after we started hanging out, we both decided that we were going back to BUD/S and we were going to graduate.

Returning to BUD/S is not quite as easy as going the first time. It would basically take an act of Congress to have the opportunity to try again. We would have to put what they called a "package" together and send it to DC for approval. This was a long process because it would require a ton of signatures. We did absolutely everything everyone told us to do. I joined the honor guard to help improve my evaluations. We would train with the explosive ordnance disposal (EOD) detachment there, and we did any odd jobs they did not want to do. I told myself that I would not drink until I made it through Hell Week, and I quit smoking altogether.

Cue the Rocky soundtrack. Dennis and I trained our butts off. We would run, no matter what the weather. We bought elastic cleats for our shoes so we could run in three feet of snow and ice. We would go to the base pool and swim for hours sometimes. We would often swim with fins to get our feet used to them.

We were very diligent in our diet. In fact, there would be times that we would fast. Dennis did it primarily for spiritual reasons, and I guess I did too. But it made me focus like I have never focused before. We joined the base wrestling team, and because we did so well, the Navy flew us to Norfolk to try out for the Navy wrestling team. Dennis was a much better wrestler than me. I think he actually was offered a position but turned it down because it would have kept him from going to SEAL training.

The day came when we finally received our orders. Our packages had been approved and we were going back to BUD/S!

CHAPTER 11

Coronado, California (Round 2)

After leaving Iceland, I went back to Austin to pick up my car from my parents' house. My dad had shown interest in accompanying me on the drive out to California. I had no problem with that at all, so we packed everything up in the car and headed out west.

Dad took the first shift behind the wheel. On the way to I-10 West we passed a sign that said the jackpot in the Texas lottery was over a hundred million dollars. I looked at dad and said, "You know, we should pull over and get a ticket."

His eyes stayed on the road as he asked me, "What would you buy with all that money?"

This question excited me. "Hmm…" I said with my mouth closed and my hand stroking an imaginary beard. "Are you kidding? I would buy whatever I wanted; I would travel to wherever I wanted. It would be awesome!"

He turned for a second to look at me and gave me a smile before putting his eyes back on the road. "What would you want after you had bought everything, and traveled everywhere you wanted to go?"

This question actually kind of stumped me. Like I have said many times, my dad is an intelligent man, and I knew he was leading somewhere. "I don't know, dad. Where are you going with that?"

He looked up to check the rear view mirror before his response, "I bet that after you had bought everything, travelled, and bought more stuff, there would be something that you would want more than anything."

I stared at him with my curiosity piqued.

He went on, "You would desire what you actually have right now."

I remember my initial thought being, "What the hell is he talking about?" But as I thought about it, it started to make a little bit of sense.

It would be many years before I fully grasped what he meant by that comment. He was absolutely right, though. I often have to remind myself of that conversation even now. Money does not make you happy or solve every problem you'll face; it is struggle, determination, and perseverance, that bring you reward. Any success is an illusion without sacrifice or failure.

I am not saying that financial success is the devil, but I believe it should serve like an odometer—a tool to show how hard the car has worked. And just like in a car, it should never be the most important gauge to look at. Other things are a hundred times more important than mileage. The value of a machine does not rest entirely on its efficiency or productivity, but also on what it produces and where you let it take you. The type of father or mother, or husband or wife a person is, and that person's relationship with his or her Creator far outweighs the value of wealth. I know how counterintuitive this can be to understand—especially when our society uses money and fame to measure success. But it all comes down to one's name. The tough decisions, the sacrifices, the struggle, and the love and compassion a person shows are what bring meaning and life to one's name. Nothing else from this world except that name will follow a person to the grave.

Even as a kid living in Egypt, I sensed this. Walking through the Museum of Cairo and looking at all the treasures uncovered from the royal tombs, I would laugh to myself imagining a ghost pharaoh somewhere wondering where the hell all his shit had gone.

As we made our way toward Tucson, we started to see signs for the "Thing." I remember these stupid signs from my last drive to California. They were around even when we were children. I remember going on a road trip somewhere with my brother and sister, and us begging our parents to pull over and let us see the "Thing". These signs littered almost the whole stretch of I-10 leading to Tucson.

After about the tenth sign I looked at my dad and said, "I can't go my whole life without knowing what the damn thing is, dad."

He laughed and, looking at the gas gauge, said, "We will need gas by the time we get to that exit." We pulled in to the gas station that was next to the large building that had the "Thing" in it, filled up the car, and made our way inside. It was full of all kinds of touristy crap—paperweights with scorpions sealed in some kind of clear polymer, turquoise jewelry, T-shirts, hats, etc. We made our way to the counter and asked the attendant about the "Thing." He told us it was eight dollars a person to check it out. Dad paid the man, and he pointed to a door in the back of the store. We walked back there and he pushed a button opening it for us. We walked inside.

I imagine you might be wondering what the "Thing" was. Well, you could send me eight bucks and I'd tell you, or you could drive all the way out to the middle of nowhere Arizona, pay your eight dollars, and see it for yourself.

Our plan was to link up with Dennis in Tucson. Dennis and his mother had also decided to take the trip together. We ended up meeting them at a motel somewhere in Tucson where they had spent the night.

I had heard Dennis talk about his pride and joy for almost a year while we were in Iceland. As we pulled into the parking lot there was no mistaking his car. It was a beautiful black and yellow muscle car from the 1980's. I wish I could remember the exact year and model, but if I got it wrong I would never hear the end of it. I think it was a Camaro, though. It's funny that I remember this, but Dennis insisted on putting it through the car wash before we took off.

We all had lunch and then hit the road. As we drove up through the mountains that would take us into California, I remember feeling anxious, excited, and reserved about what was awaiting me ahead. Looking out the window, I thought about how miserable I was in Iceland and what I had done to myself the first year there. I could not ever let that happen again—ever!

We finally arrived and checked into the quarterdeck. In that lobby they had a book that had every class picture from every BUD/S class over the years. We looked at it and I saw class 201's picture. I remembered how we'd started with so many guys as I saw so few of them standing in that picture.

Dennis saw me looking at my old class and said, "Our pictures are going to be in this book, Brett." That brought a smile to my face because I knew I was ready for the fight.

The events leading up to Hell Week happened just as they had before, except with one small difference. I became the gray man. This was the guy who was not the slowest guy, but was also not the fastest. The instructors did not have my name committed to memory. This made me a very happy person. Dennis, on the other hand, was a freaking stud. He came in first in almost everything.

One day a week we had to run the obstacle course for time. I remember watching Dennis start his run after I had finished. There was an obstacle called the Dirty Name. We would start on a log about two and half feet above the ground. Then we had to leap to a log that was about seven and a half feet high and three feet away. Finally, there was another log that was twelve and a half feet high and another three feet away. The obstacle got its name from how it felt jumping from log to log. We had to actually catch the log by the stomach to be able to crawl on top of it and jump to the last one.

Dennis jumped from the first log to the second, actually landing one foot above it. He then pushed off of it, almost springing him over the top of the last log, which he would grab on his way over to help slow his fall to the ground. It was amazing to actually watch. He would come very close many times to setting a new record on that obstacle course.

By the weekend before Hell Week, I had done a really good job on staying on top of my injuries. Those weeks are very rough on the body, and instead of taking the moments I had to rest, I focused on stretching and icing everything that I could. I remember having a serious case of shin splints, and in-between physical evolutions I would massage and ice them.

Sunday morning came and I remember seeing a report on The Weather Channel about a hurricane approaching San Diego. The berms had been built up to around twenty-five feet high along the beach in preparation for the storm. I remember not really caring about it, but being more concerned about having to carry logs and boats over those berms for the next week.

Nighttime came and I found myself on the beach in an old Army tent, waiting for break out. The first explosion went off and it was go time. Everything happened just like I remembered it from the first time.

Not long after, we once again found ourselves being surf tortured in the frigid Pacific Ocean. A couple hours went by and I remember the first guy leaving. I remember calling out to him with the rest of my class. Lots of guys had already quit in weeks leading up to this point, but it was that guy I remembered the most because I'd known that guy two years before.

After what seemed like an eternity, the instructors called us out of the water and had us do a four mile timed run. During that run I was so excited that I had made it past that first test. But the week was far from over, and there would be many, many more trials to come.

Not long after that we grabbed our IBS's, or inflatable boat (small)'s. Each boat crew had their own boat. We had used these boats a lot leading up to Hell Week. Sometimes the instructors would have us paddle them out past the surf zone and then paddle them back in—often to their amusement, depending on how high and powerful the waves were. As long as it was not my boat crew, I even found myself laughing as I watched other crews get flipped and thrown from their boats. It would become a circus trying to flip the boat over, get everyone back into it, and start paddling again—all while the waves mercilessly pounded away.

We would end up taking those damn boats everywhere with us that week. Each of them weighed 108 lbs. when they were dry, but were rarely ever free of sand and water. The easiest way to carry a boat was with everybody putting his head under it; three guys on each side and one in the back. There was a slight raise in the boat toward the rear, which meant more headroom for whoever held that position. A good boat crew leader would rotate his position in the back. My favorite crew leaders would put the smallest person, whose head barely touched the boat, in that spot most of the time, ensuring that the greatest number of load bearers were under that boat. The most hated crew leaders would never leave that position.

The first night all we did was run from one torturing station to another with those boats on our heads. And everything was always, always a race. Everyone was constantly getting sent to the surf to get wet and sandy. The winner of any given event was awarded a few minutes of rest while everybody else was punished. It was a long, cold, miserable night.

The dark sky got lighter and lighter, and all I could think about was that sun coming up and the warmth it would bring. It finally rose and we ran to the chow hall with our boats on our heads to eat breakfast. We staged the boats outside in the parking lot, posting one person from each crew to stand guard over his boat. This he would do in the parade rest position (standing at attention with one hand in the small of the back and the other holding a paddle upright). Halfway through the meal we would rotate another guy out to allow everyone to eat.

After breakfast we ran back to the compound to get checked out by medical. This involved a quick stripping down of all our clothes, and walking through an assembly line of sorts. A doctor would look for injuries. It was early in the game, so most guys just had rashes from where the sand would stick to their wet pants and shirts—especially in the crotch and armpits. At the next station a corpsman, keeping his distance, would spray our dicks or anywhere else these rashes were developing with some kind of disinfectant from a window cleaning bottle. Then we would move on to the foot guy, who would check our feet for anything out of the ordinary. I would come to love the foot guys because they were all corpsman that were in PTRR waiting to class up. When instructors were not looking, they would massage our feet or slip us some ibuprofen. After the medical screening we would get dressed as fast as we could and run back out to the beach to join the rest of the class.

The days were difficult. We were always wet, and constantly doing something tough and miserable. But I found that it was easy for me to zone out during the day.

After dinner, we were doing something that involved us running back and forth from the beach to the water, and I remember an instructor getting on a PA system in his truck and saying, "Say goodbye to the sun, gents!"

I dreaded the thought of the sun going down. Shit got real when the sun went down.

The sun slowly started dipping below the water.

"It's not too late, I have hot coffee and doughnuts in my truck for the next quitter."

Not long after that, somebody took him up on his offer. I remember us doing a lot more of my favorite thing that night... surf torture. I found that if I just focused on making it through that particular evolution, I could allow myself to consider quitting afterwards if I wanted. Somehow that thought helped me make it through those difficult times.

By Tuesday morning, we had lost about fifteen to twenty guys. We were constantly switching boat crews as people quit. Boats would be taken away, and we would be shifted to crews that were missing people. Tuesday was just like the day before—full of long beat downs, carrying logs, racing with boats... it just went on and on. We never got dry.

I knew that night was going to be especially tough. I had heard many stories from the guys who had finished Hell Week about a thing called the "steel pier." It sounded miserable. The instructors would make us strip down to our underwear, lie on a very cold steel barge, and spray us with a hose until enough people quit. As the sun was setting I remember praying that God would help me out that night.

Eventually, we made our way out to the pier. Already cold and miserable, the instructors had us strip down to our underwear and lay on that cold slab of steel. Time came to a screeching halt. Every minute felt like an hour, and every hour was an eternity. People started to quit, and we would try to cheer them back. I remember we all started singing at one point, which seemed to help a little.

The slab was slightly angled, which allowed water to run off the barge. At one point, the guy behind me started to take a piss, and it ran down to me and under my back. It was so warm and felt so good. I turned my head up to him and said, "I will pay you a dollar if you do that again." He laughed.

Dismally long hours skulked by. Then it happened; while staring up in the dark night sky the unmistakable comfort of the horizon getting lighter came into view. Somehow I made it through that night.

The next morning in the chow hall, I could see on a TV (before the instructors turned it off) what looked like a giant red blob right off the coast of California. It was the hurricane. It made my heart sink in my chest. My sun was going to leave.

During our medical check that morning, things were starting to get serious. Rashes were getting severe, there were blisters on feet, and some guys were developing blisters on the tops of their heads from the boat rubbing and bouncing on it all the time. As I made my way through the assembly line, I couldn't help but notice the guy in front of me. The head of his dick was so swollen from the constant rubbing against sandy clothes that it looked like small red apple being held to his body by a finger. I looked up at him and asked, "Does it hurt?"

He looked at me and said sarcastically, "What do you think, Jones?" I saw his face cringe as the corpsman sprayed an extra amount of disinfectant on that thing.

Before we were done with medical, the clouds had rolled in and it was starting to drizzle. Throughout the day, the weather would slowly worsen. The waves were starting to get big, and the wind was picking up. However, the day continued on just like the previous ones.

That night the waves had turned into monsters. From the beach, we really could not see them because of the rain and how overcast it was, and because they were breaking about a hundred yards out. But we certainly could hear them.

The instructors had us pile into our boats and do what is called "surf passage." As a boat crew, everyone paddles out to the point just before the waves break. Once a wave broke, we would paddle like hell over the remaining white water until we'd cleared the incoming swells.

As we were paddling out, our boat crew leader was casually giving the command "Stroke... stroke... stoke..." This went on until we got to the spot just before the waves were crashing. They were so thunderous as we made our way out. Oddly enough, in the direction the waves were coming from the clouds had broken apart in a portion of the sky, revealing stars.

A wave crashed down in front of us, and we began to paddle as hard and as fast as we could. The boat crew leader was now yelling, "Stroke! Stroke! Stroke! Stroke!" Being in the front of the boat, I struggled like hell to keep up with his cadence, along with everyone else. I was trying my hardest while I paddled to try and see the incoming wave. It was just too dark. Instead, I focused on my little break in the clouds. I soon saw the stars start to disappear, but not from the clouds.

I yelled, "Holy fuck! Paddle faster!" The last thing I remember seeing was our boat being completely vertical. I was looking down at the rest of the crew, and then came the immense feeling of being thrown. Finally, something hit my head. I am not sure if it was the boat or a sand bar, but it knocked me out.

I remember coming back to consciousness, only to be hit by another wave. A buddy swam over to me, grabbed my life preserver and swam me to shore.

"Jonsey, are you OK?" he asked.

I remember feeling quite calm, almost like I'd just gotten my reset button pushed. "I feel okay" I slowly mumbled.

The instructors immediately ran out to the waist-deep water where I now was. They took me and put me on a stretcher with a spinal collar brace. Shining flashlights in my eyes, they put me in the back of an ambulance that had been staged on the beach. I remember telling them that I was okay and to please let me go back to my class. They drove me out to Balboa Hospital in San Diego, where I was immediately rushed into an x-ray machine.

Twenty minutes later, a female doctor comes out and tells me, "Well, nothing is broken."

Thirty minutes later, I was back with my class, thanking God that I was allowed to continue. However, I had to pay the man big time when I got back from that little vacation. My next few meals were exceptionally brief. Instead, I spent that time being hosed down while everyone else was in the warm cafeteria. This adventure had also bought me a ticket on the chain gang, which was something like the goon squad, only it came during the fun of Hell Week.

I don't remember a lot from Wednesday night on—it all kind of blurs together. Those of us who were left had become drones. I remember getting to the point where I'd become a zombie. I just did was I was told to do. I have memories of hallucinating faces in trees, and being extremely cold but somehow just not caring anymore. I vaguely remember a talent show we had to do for the instructors before the sun came up. I sang an opera song, much to their amusement, and somehow we won five minutes in a hot shower because of that.

Thursday night came, and we started the night by paddling around the entire peninsula of Coronado. The instructors would meet us at different points. Between checkpoints we actually got moderately dry. Like everything else it was a race, and it paid to be a winner.

Things started getting really weird. We all started hallucinating the weirdest shit. I remember one guy telling us to look out for a whale he thought was in the water. Somehow, it made us all think we kept seeing a whale swimming under us. Guys would often fall asleep and then fall off the side of the boat. Somehow I managed to not fall in, though I came close several times.

At another point, the instructors put us in a classroom that had the heat turned way up high and then gave us twenty minutes to write an essay on why we wanted to be a SEAL. They would pull out anyone who fell asleep and he would end up in the drink. I remember focusing on staying awake because I liked being warm, but for the life of me I can't recall what I wrote. I do know that whenever I started to fade out my pen would start making a squiggly line. When I finished my paper it looked like hiero-glyphics or something. I never did get to see what I wrote.

Then Friday morning came, and I was just hours from hearing those four magic words, "Hell Week is secured!" By this time, the storm had passed and the sun was out. It felt so good to see the sun again.

We all headed out to a place called the demo pit—a giant mud pit with two ropes going across it, one above the other. The instructors threw smoke grenades around the pit while we all sat in the mud at the bottom of the ten-foot hole. One by one, we all tried to cross it, standing on one line and holding the other above our heads while the instructors on either end violently shook the ropes. Of course, nobody made it across. But some of the wipeouts were epic and hilarious.

We ate a box lunch in the mud of that pit and then made our way to our boats to paddle back to the compound. We all rode giant waves back into the beach and then ran into the grinder.

Eventually, the commanding officer gave the command we had all been waiting for. It was about two or three in the afternoon.

Up to this point we all had to wear white T-shirts with our names stenciled on them under our uniforms. Those who fin-ished Hell Week were given brown ones. There was a table waiting for us by the barracks with a pizza, a large Gatorade, and a brown T-shirt with our names on them. It was an awe-some feeling.

After eating our pizza and telling each other about some funny things that had happened to us, we made our way to our rooms. The most sleep anybody had gotten through the entire week was about two hours. The mattresses from the top bunks were on the ground, and a large bag was at the foot of each one. We got into our beds, and put our feet on the bags to prevent swelling, then went on what I like to call a spiritual journey.

A corpsman constantly monitored us while we slept. Guys would walk in their sleep. Others would piss themselves, because that was what we'd done all week. There was definitely no shortage of guys talking in their sleep. As for me, I remember dreaming that I couldn't keep my boat over my head because it was deflated. Instructors were screaming at me to get it above my head. I woke up sweating, trying to push my blanket above me. I got up to use the bathroom once, but after that I did not wake up again until three p.m. the next day. I dreamed about Hell Week the entire time. The next day I felt like I had been eaten by a werewolf and shit down the side of a cliff.

On Saturday night some of us went to Outback Steakhouse. It was the first time I had ever been there. I ordered the biggest steak and a giant ice-cold Foster's beer. When my food arrived, it smelled like the air occupying the low-pressure area created by an angel beating its wings. It was beyond good, it was deserved.

While we were eating, Mark McGrath from the band Sugar Ray was having dinner a couple tables away. At the time, none of us knew or cared who he was, but our waitress sure did because she would come over and tell us every five minutes what he was doing. She had a pretty, girl-next-door kind of face, with long dirty-blonde, almost brown, hair. She also had rather large breasts, and was not afraid to rest them on our shoulders as she removed or placed items on the table. It was amusing to watch guys finish their drinks quickly so that she would bring another one. The smiles would be from ear to ear every time she rested those large, warm bosoms on someone. We would all tell stories about the past week, and I laughed so hard that my stomach muscles would hurt. I remember the way we looked walking out. Everyone walked bow-legged, like they were eighty years old. Outback is to this day one of my all-time favorite restaurants, if not my favorite. Every time I go in one it reminds me of how I felt the night after finishing by far the toughest week of my life.

BUD/S was far from over, and it was right back to work on Monday. The next week was spent mostly in the classroom. To allow our feet to breathe and heal, we did not have to wear our boots for a couple of days.

The classes were all about hydro reconnaissance, stalking, creating situational reports, and mission planning. The last week of first phase was spent actually going out and practicing those skills. There would still be beatings, and getting wet and sandy. But the instructors had a little more respect for us at this point, and most of the time they would only bring the pain if we screwed up.

Second phase started with a briefing from the lieutenant in charge of that phase. There were going to be a few hurdles in this phase. First was getting through dive physics, and then came a thing called pool comp, and after that was a five nautical mile ocean swim. And of course we could not fail any of the timed events, like the four mile timed runs, two mile timed ocean swims, or the timed obstacle courses. The timed events were going to be more difficult in second phase because the minimum passing times required became shorter in each phase of training.

The dive physics classes were fairly difficult for me at the time. At night one of the officers who had graduated from the Naval Academy would help me study. Ensign Woody was from Boston, or somewhere close to it—there was no mistaking his accent. He was one of the boat crew leaders I really liked. Anyway, he understood how frustrating all the formulas and equations were for me.

We would all have to pass a written exam before we moved on in training. Enlisted guys had to just get a grade of seventy or above, whereas officers were held to the higher standard of eighty or above. Surprisingly enough, I received an eighty-eight on that test. I actually got a higher score than Woody did.

We first learned how to scuba dive on the old double hose regulators. They had an inhalation hose and an exhalation hose that linked up to a regulator located on the top of the twin 80 scuba tanks. On our first dive the instructors had us practice swimming in circles around the pool. It felt like flying, and it was fun.

After we'd done a couple laps and were getting familiar with it, we all had to tread water with no fins and just the tanks strapped to our backs. It started to remind me of the beehive because it was a fight to stay alive. By the end of that miserable five minutes my fingers and toes were numb. Since I was one of the first guys to go, it was nice to relax and watch others have to do it. I know it sounds terrible, but somehow watching other guys suffer the same way that I had was quite amusing.

Before we could move on to the advanced form of re-breathing diving we would have to get through a thing called pool comp. You would only get two tries at it, and then you could get dropped from the program or rolled back to the next class.

Pool comp was designed to see how well we could memorize a series of procedures underwater in stressful conditions. By stressful I mean that instructors were constantly fucking with us while we wore blacked-out masks underwater.

The day quickly arrived, and I had stayed up most of the night practicing my procedures over and over. I went over them in my head many times, even on my way to the pool.

We lined up on the side of the pool with our backs to the water so we could not watch what was going on there. I was the fifth guy up in the line, and they were only doing one guy at a time. Once we finished, we would come to the surface and yell, "I feel fine." This let the instructors know we were okay.

The first guy was down under the water for almost twenty minutes. Again, while I was waiting, I would just go over in my mind every procedure. I heard a loud splashing noise followed by a gargled and exhausted, "I feel fine!"

The instructors in the pool yelled to another instructor recording results on a clipboard, "This one is a fail!" They had him sit on the other side of the pool, to keep from talking to or warning us of what happened under the water. For almost the next two hours that was all I heard: "Fail!"

Everybody was failing. I was starting to get extremely nervous.

It was now my turn. I got into the water and swam over to the middle of the deep end where the instructors were. There were three in the water with me. The one closest to me asked if I was ready and I gave him the thumbs up. Before I went under he told me, "Just relax, and you'll be fine."

I allowed myself to sink to the bottom, where I stayed on my knees. I could not see anything with the blacked-out mask on. I relaxed and started singing a song in my head.

All of a sudden, I could not inhale. I felt somebody doing something to my tanks. Then I stopped being able to breath.

Quickly, I went through the procedure and fixed the problem. Not long after that I felt all three of them throwing me around. Again, I went through my procedures to fix problems and get my gear working again.

All of a sudden, right as I exhaled, they took my mouthpiece. I relaxed and waited for them to stop doing whatever it was they were doing. When I felt no more moving, I knew it was time to get back to work.

I was going to have to be quick this time, because I could tell the panic was not far away. I found my mouthpiece and tried to suck in air… nothing. I reached back and turned the air on. I sucked in. A mixture of air and water came, and I inhaled both. My first instinct was to cough; I would have to prevent myself from doing that, because it would create more problems by causing me to inhale more water.

The panic had set in.

I had three problems now—controlling the panic, keeping myself from coughing, and figuring out why water was coming in and fixing that problem.

Somehow, I was able to slowly inhale oxygen with my head facing the floor pulling the air and water to the roof of my mouth and somewhat separating the two with my tongue. This allowed me to exhale the water through the exhalation hose. This process gave just enough of the air I needed to keep me from passing out. It was not a perfect process because I would still breathe in drops of water, but it bought me time while I went through the procedures for my inhalation problem.

Finally, they gave me the impossible problem. One would try to work it out, but would have to know beyond a doubt what was the case. They did it to me, and I went through everything twice. Going through the correct order of operations was a time consuming process. I could not breathe at all at this point and was experiencing acute panic inside my body and was moments from being unconscious. There was nothing more I could physically do.

Then I gave the signal and slowly came to the surface, blowing what remained of my air out. I got to the surface and yelled "I feel fine!" followed by a coughing fit to push the water out of my lungs, with loud gagging noises between the coughs.

The instructors, laughing, yelled, "Pass!"

I thought to myself, "Thank God," 'cause there was no way in hell I wanted to do that again. Only a few of us passed that day. The rest would have one more shot at it the next day. We ended up losing two or three guys as a result of pool comp.

Next we moved on to the rebreathing systems. Think of this as diving with no bubbles. It was a more difficult form of diving, but it enabled a diver to stay underwater much longer and be stealthy. We would move on to navigating underwater, how to plan dives, and how to put mines on ships. There was a ton of diving involved, and most of it was done at night in the bay.

The day came for us to do the five nautical mile ocean swim. We met on the beach early in the morning, went through a swimmer's inspection, and then into the water we went. For any dive or ocean swim we would have a swim buddy who was close to an equivalent level in swimming. This would allow both swimmers to get the best possible swim time. Today's swim was not for time, though; we just had to complete it.

This was an El Nino year, and the currents were all jacked up. It took my swim buddy and me about four and a half hours to finish it, and we were the fourth team to finish. During the swim we would use a combat swimmer sidestroke, which is basically a sidestroke in which the only part of the body that comes above the water is one's head. We would swim like this facing each other, and occasionally one of us would look ahead to make sure that we were on course. We would take a break about once every hour to switch sides and talk for about a minute about how fucking miserable it was and how it seemed like we were not moving very fast. Our reward for finishing was that we both found ourselves extremely nauseous for a couple hours afterwards due to the amount of seawater we unconsciously drank.

Second phase came to an end, and somehow I had managed to pass all my times. However, I knew going into third phase that I was going to have some issues with the four-mile timed run. I was barely passing them in second phase, and they were about to drop a whole minute off the required time.

Third phase—the land warfare phase—would end up being around seven weeks long. We would learn basic weapons, demolitions, land navigation, patrolling, marksmanship, and small unit tactics. We would drive up to the mountains for a week to work on our land navigation, and then for the last three weeks of training we would fly out to a remote island off the coast of California to practice all those things.

We jumped right into land navigation and weapons training. The classes were long, and so were the practical exercises. We would still get into trouble with the instructors from time to time, but now they were starting to treat us like humans and were really focused on teaching us the skills we would need to become good operators in the SEAL teams. I really enjoyed this part of the training. I discovered that I was an above-average shooter in my class, and sailed through the training.

Three days before our class was scheduled to go to the island, we had to do another four mile timed run. If I did not pass this run, I would not be going to the island. Failing it meant risking the chance of being dropped from the whole course if they decided to not let me go through that phase of training again with the next class.

It was early and the sun had not come up yet. We stood at the starting line looking at the instructors. They gave us the go ahead and we were off. I ran as hard I possibly could. It had not rained in a while, so the sand was very dry and especially difficult that day; my feet felt like they were sinking six inches into it with every step I took.

I failed that run by eight seconds.

I was crushed. I was only three weeks from graduating!

That afternoon I went before a review board. They would decide whether or not I would be dropped or rolled back into the next class. They asked me a bunch of questions and then dismissed me from the office. I stood outside that office for about ten minutes, praying that I would not get dropped. Finally, one of the instructors on the board yelled, "Get back in here, Jones!"

I walked in and the commander said, "I am going to roll you to the next class. You have been a good student, and looking at your record I can tell that you want this. You'd better spend the time waiting for the next class becoming a runner."

I smiled and said, "Yes, sir. Thank you very much, sir."

For the next month I did just as he said. I bought running magazines and books. I focused all of my attention on becoming a good runner. One of the books talked about visualization. Lying in bed at night, I would go through an entire four mile run in my head, step by step, before going out and running it the next day. In my mind, I would focus on my breathing and staying calm while I ran very quickly. I would also imagine that running fast for that long was easy for me, and that it was enjoyable passing other students.

A month or so later, I found myself starting third phase all over again. Before long I was right back at that starting line again. I started in the back of the pack because passing people gave me motivation somehow. My new class was down to about seventeen people, and I remember being the fifth one to cross the finish line.

It was a good day; I had no doubt that I was going to graduate in three weeks.

We all flew out to the island, and we all faced many different challenges out there. There would be a fourteen-mile run, a road march, tons of shooting, and lots of blowing shit up—hell yeah! The days were long, and we got just a few hours of sleep a night, but it all paid off.

A couple of hours before graduation, our entire class attended the spreading of the ashes of a Navy SEAL. It had been his wish in his old age that his ashes be spread in the surf zone behind the compound, with a graduating class to witness his remains' return to the sea. We all lined the berm, standing at attention in our dress uniforms, while his wife and an old friend of his poured the ashes into the surf. A strong wind blew at that very moment and carried some of his ashes onto the class. Seeing the approaching cloud, I held my breath and squinted my eyes. Afterwards, I looked on my uniform and could see the slightest remnants of him. I left it alone. I figured he just wanted to be a part of it again.

It was now graduation time, and my entire family showed up for the ceremony. They held the ceremony in the movie theater on the other side of the base. I remember the pride I felt as I crossed the stage, got my graduation certificate, and returned to my class which only had 12 original guys left in it.

After the ceremony, I had the honor to meet Fred (Tiz) Morrison, the very first black Navy SEAL. He had a small teddy bear in his arm, and told me that his granddaughter had given it to him. I thought it was picture-perfect, because he didn't care what anybody thought about a grown man carrying around a teddy bear amongst a roomful of SEALs. As I shook his hand, he gave me a sincere smile and congratulated me. Not many people knew he was there. If it had not been for my father talking to him, I would have missed out on that once in a lifetime opportunity. I was a very lucky person to meet such an important historical figure before he passed away. He was a brave man. He never had the luxury of hiding the fact he was black.

It was just so much to take in! This was undoubtedly the happiest day of my life. The crisp white of our uniforms, the brilliant colors of the American flags everywhere, and even the awesome weather that day are just as clear in my mind as if it had happened yesterday.

I had come to know what true friendship was, and what it really meant to be a friend. We had a saying, "I trust you with my life, but not my money or my wife." I trusted them with my life, as they did me, and we had proven that to each other countless times. If there was any doubt whether I was still floating somewhere between being a boy and a man, it was forever erased that day.

CHAPTER 12

SEAL Team 8

After BUD/S, I went to the Army's Airborne School for three weeks before heading to Seal Team 8 in Virginia Beach, VA. Once I'd joined my team, I spent the next four months going through SEAL tactical training and studying for my Trident Board.

The Trident Board was a group of seasoned SEALS who would bring you into a conference room full of completely disassembled weapons, communications equipment, and navigational tools and maps. You would spend 3-6 hours in that room answering any question or demonstrating your knowledge of the equipment. It was incredibly stressful. Often you found yourself doing multiple things at once while answering questions. After it concluded they would take a vote to see if you were ready to receive your Trident.

The SEAL trident is the pin that you wear on your uniform symbolizing you're an actual SEAL. It's the largest pin on your uniform. It depicts a gold eagle with his wings spread holding a trident in one claw and a flintlock style pistol in the other crossed over an anchor in the center. It is meant to represent the type of combat a SEAL is capable of (sea, air, and land warfare).

After successfully passing the board, I was given my SEAL Trident by the commanding officer of SEAL Team 8 in front of the entire team and our support staff. That was the day I officially became a Navy SEAL.

In true Nordic fashion the brotherhood welcomed me with friendly punches to my chest were my trident now rested and a keg of beer.

It really was a significant moment. I felt like I was finally a part of something incredibly rare, something worth taking the hard road. I was one of them now.

I am not going to say that I slept in that uniform that night because that is just weird, but I am not going to deny it either.

Soon after that I found myself assigned to a platoon. A platoon consisted of fourteen to sixteen guys. These men would become family. We would spend the next eighteen months training our asses off together. If I was not training with them, I was probably at a school. The schools were essential to becoming a better operator. There were schools to become a sniper, a breacher (demolitions expert for gaining entry into places), a lead climber, a jumpmaster, a high altitude low opening parachutist (HALO), and many more. The more skills a SEAL had, the more valuable he became to the platoon and the team.

The SEAL community is a very small one. In fact, one has a much better chance of meeting an NFL player than an actual SEAL. Being that it is such a small community, each SEAL constantly has to prove his worth to the team. It is the most competitive environment that I have ever witnessed or even heard of in my life, and I loved it.

The idea that the hard days are over after graduation is complete crap. Each SEAL is constantly being judged by the team. Everything from one's physical condition, to marksmanship, to communication, to one's form when diving—it just goes on and on. SEALs who do just enough to get by find themselves at the top of the gossip network. Once someone is labeled a "shit bag," it is a tough road back to redemption.

SEALs, as a whole, are a good-looking, in-shape group of guys. A lot of my gay friends ask me about working in that environment and being gay. I can see that their imaginations are running wild with scenes of group showers, naked guys in locker rooms, or having to sleep next to each other for warmth. To their disappointment I explain that, though these things do happen, they are not homoerotic things. The bond that is created between a SEAL and his brothers is a sacred one.

The Special Operations community, as a whole, shares a type of espirit de corps that is inimitable. Imagine an environment where the only structure of rank is seemingly based off of experience. Where there is a deeply shared desire not only to improve yourself but your team as well. It is a community where having trust becomes as taken for granted as the need for air.

We leave no one behind.

Really think about that statement. Think of all the possible scenarios. Never leaving a buddy behind, no matter what the odds or situation... even at the price of your mortality. It's a very rare and powerful love that transcends the physical.

There are SEALs that I have found to be really attractive. However, the thought of any sexual relationship seemed incestuous to me, not to mention completely unprofessional.

I had never met or heard of a gay Navy SEAL. People find that hard to believe. The law of averages says that there are others, and I hope that's the case. I don't envy them, though, for their role is much more difficult now. They have to be the example, and lead the way towards creating the proper atmosphere of acceptance in the community—especially now that the "Don't ask, don't tell" policy is in the shit pile of bad ideas, where it belongs.

CHAPTER 13

North Arabian Gulf

After the long eighteen-month work-up, I found myself right where I'd always dreamed I would be. The two combat speedboats were going so fast they would skip over the slightest bump in the water. The sea was very smooth, the sky was clear, and the slivered moon hung above the horizon.

Even at night, the air was heavy and warm in that part of the world, but we could hardly notice it gliding across the water as fast as we were. Looking over my right shoulder I could see the wake left by the other boat two hundred feet away, carrying the other half of my platoon. Behind us I could hear the Blackhawk in close pursuit, with one of our snipers on board.

This was the night. All my training had led up to this point. Somewhere out in that vast darkness ahead there was a tanker smuggling oil from Iraq to help fund the Iraqi military. The ship was moving into international waters because its draft was too deep, forcing it further out to sea. We had a very limited time to take control of it and its crew before it slipped into Iranian waters.

I could feel my heart beating. This was no longer a training exercise. There were not going to be any "time outs" to discuss alternatives. This was the real deal, and I was constantly going over, and over, and over it in my head.

I was one of two breachers. It was my job to get us through anything that kept us from getting inside and taking control of the ship. I was nervous because I was not allowed to use explosives. During the planning process the team decided it was too much of a risk because of the large oil cargo. This put me at a great disadvantage.

The other breacher had a plasma torch. I had bolt cutters, a sledgehammer, a quickie saw, and a hooligan tool, which is similar to a crow bar but with a sharp pike that sticks out on one side. These tools were great for houses, but not for metal ships. Ship hatches are a unique beast; they are like the door on a safe. Being unable to use explosives, I knew I was in for a challenge if the plasma torch failed.

The plan was pretty simple. One team boards and takes control of the bridge, the other searches the ship and takes control of the crew. Meanwhile, a sniper hovers above to take out any threats during the process.

Suddenly, there it was. I could see the back of the five-story superstructure located on the stern of the large, dilapidated ship. It looked like a ghost ship, with not a soul in sight.

"We are hot," the platoon commander announced in my earpiece. The boats gunned it. The sniper flew around to the port side of the ship, hovering perfectly in place. The helicopter's pilots matched the speed and direction of the ship to allow the sniper cleaner shots.

The ship was so laden with oil that water was actually cresting over the main deck. I found some relief in this, because scaling a ship with the hook and ladders is an exhausting task with the amount of equipment I had.

We literally stepped onto the ship as a platoon and made our way to the superstructure. The main deck was covered in water and rusted, with jagged edges everywhere we looked. Once we arrived at the first stairwell going up, we broke off into two fire teams.

Other than the sound of the helicopter, everything was very quiet and dark. Looking around, I noticed the Iraqis had turned this ship into a tank. Every window had a steel plate welded to it, and all the hatches had been welded shut.

"Holy shit, they were expecting us," I thought as we made our way around the structure to find some prospect of entry.

"There has to be a way they get in and out of there," our commander said. "Break into two-man groups to search for a way in."

The breacher on the bridge was having no luck with the torch. The turbulent rotor wash from the Blackhawk kept putting out his lighters. He only had three chances to light the torch, and was not able to make it happen.

"Jonesy, come to the back of the superstructure," my platoon commander ordered over the radio. We cleared our way back to his location. "This is the only door not welded. Get us in there!"

"Roger that," I whispered.

I immediately went to read the door while the other guys pulled security around me. Looking at it made my heart sink in my chest. It was an outward-opening, thick metal hatch.

"Think, Brett... think! I only have fucking manual tools! The saw would take forever to use on something like this," I thought to myself.

The clock was ticking, and I could feel every second that I was not working on that door.

"What is the weakest part of this door, Brett? The hinges! Okay... time to make this happen!"

There were two large metal hinges to this steel hatch. They both had heavy-duty steel pins holding them together. As fast as I could, I slung my gun behind me and grabbed the bolt cutters from my backpack. I cut the slightly exposed bottom-beveled piece off both hinge pins. I would have cut the top, but it was too flush for the bolt cutters to grip anything. The pins were so damn thick! It took every bit of strength that I had, but I made it happen.

Reaching on my back, I grabbed my hooligan tool and sledgehammer. I grabbed one of the guys and told him to hold the pointed end of the hooligan under the top pin where I'd just cut off the bevel. I used the sledge to hit the hooligan, which in turn would push the pin up. I was swinging like a mad man. I could hardly breathe, and sweat was pouring from every pore in my body when I finally broke the first hinge free. We immediately went to work on the second hinge.

Sensing my exhaustion, the platoon commander said, "Don't give up, Brett. You can do this." That was all it took to fire my engines up into overdrive. Moments later, the last hinge broke free. The Iraqis had placed a chain on the door from the inside, which only required a quick snip with the bolt cutters, and we were inside that motherfucker in less than ten minutes!

The platoon made short work of taking control of the bridge and the crew. It was amazing! Not a single Iraqi was killed, and not one SEAL injured. Moving through the ship, our platoon was so fast and efficient that most of the crew had no idea what was happening.

I can't imagine being fast asleep in my room when, Boom! A group of Navy SEALS put me on the ground and cuffs me before I can even get a sound out of my mouth. I know it's not supposed to be funny, but I laugh every time I think about some of the expressions I saw.

That was a very meaningful day for me. It was the day I was no longer riding on the coattails of the SEAL reputation. I actually did something significant to contribute to that reputation. Though getting us through that hatch may not seem like the kind of stuff you'd find in, say, a Charlie Sheen movie, but my role not only marked the difference between success and failure, but possibly between life and death for me and my team.

CHAPTER 14

Virginia Beach, VA (Part 1)

A couple of years later, and two weeks after 9/11, my second platoon was deployed for six months. When I returned in 2002, Rick had a welcome home party for me at our house.

For the past two and a half years I had been involved in a relationship. I had met Rick at a bar in Norfolk. We dated, and it did not take long for us to buy a house together not far from the base where we both worked. Rick was also in the Navy, and had not long ago put on the rank of senior chief. He had worked as a cook for almost his entire time in the Navy. He was extremely passionate about his culinary arts, and was very good at what he did.

A few of my neighbors and gay friends had come to the welcome home party, and I spent most of my time talking to them. I had felt kind of bad because the party lasted really late, and I didn't spend as much time with Rick as I should have. I could tell I had upset him a little when we went to bed.

The next day I woke up around noon with a bit of a hangover and went to call Rick at his office. I picked up the phone and got his answering machine. I left this message: "Sorry about last night, I will make it up to you when you get home…" Just then his dog, Bubba, was at the back door pawing to get in. "Come on Bubba! Okay. I love you. Bye." Then I hung up the phone.

A couple weeks later I found myself on my way to Military Freefall School. I had waited a long time to get the opportunity to do this, and I was very excited about it. We started off at Fort Bragg, where we could practice in their wind tunnel. We stayed there for about a week before heading out to Yuma, Arizona. I was very surprised to see that one of the instructors was a guy with whom I'd gone through BUD/S. It was really nice to see him again and catch up.

We went on to Yuma and I remember very well my first freefall jump. It was nothing like jumping static line, which was done at 1,500 feet above ground level, and which involved the parachute being automatically opened by a cord attached to the aircraft. My first jump was going to be from ten thousand feet, and there was nothing automatic about deploying my parachute as I jumped from the plane.

The rear hatch of the plane slowly opened, revealing the beginning of a spectacular desert sunrise. It continued to open to a panoramic view of the mountains around Yuma. My heart was racing. From that height I could see the slight curvature of the earth to the extreme left and right. The sky was a deep, fading, cobalt blue set against the brown desert terrain that lay beneath it.

The jumpmaster looked out the back of the plane and gave me and my instructor the signal to go. I did one last check of my gear, took a deep breath, and dove out the back of the plane much like I would from the side of a pool. It took a second for the blast of air to hit me once I cleared the plane's slipstream. I was facing head-down and could see the plane below my feet. I saw my instructor jump out and start tracking towards me. Using the air rushing up towards me, I put my body in a stable position by arching my back and pushing my stomach towards the ground. This kept me from flying forwards or backwards without knowing it.

My eyes were glued to the altimeter on my wrist. I was so focused on making sure that I pulled my chute at four thousand feet that the only thing I paid attention to was that altimeter. My instructor flew over to me and tapped his finger on my goggles. I looked up at him and he pointed for me to look around with a huge smile on his face.

It was so beautiful. I could not even tell that I was falling. We were so high up at the time that it just felt like we were flying. I remember looking up at the sky and it resembling the ocean. Instead of getting darker the deeper you went, it got darker the higher I looked.

Moments later this sense of disconnect was shattered. The ground was hurling towards me. Looking at my altimeter, it was now time to pull my ripcord. It opened with a slight jolt in the straps around my crotch. I glided in and made a perfect landing. I could not wait to go again!

The course went on for the next couple weeks, each jump getting higher and with more gear. It was a blast. Before long it was the day before the last jump. One of the instructors came over to me and told me that the commanding officer of my SEAL team needed to talk to me. My mind immediately went racing. All I could think about was whether I'd done something wrong on my last deployment.

I walked into the main office building and one of the officers there stepped out of his office and told me I could use his phone. I picked up the phone and called the SEAL team, speaking briefly to somebody working the quarterdeck. He notified my commanding officer that I was calling, and transferred me to his office.

"Brett, I am not going to beat around the bush. I need you to catch a flight leaving today. There is an investigation going on, and people need to talk to you. The officer that is letting you use his phone has your plane tickets."

Confused, I replied, "What is this about, sir?"

"I can't talk about on the phone with you because of the nature of the investigation. The command master chief will pick you up from the airport."

"Yes, sir," I said. We both hung up.

It took me all of ten seconds, if that, to figure out this had nothing to do with job performance. I was a damn good SEAL, and I knew it. They had somehow figured out I was gay. My mind was a mess, I kept thinking, "There is a Don't Ask, Don't Tell policy. Why the hell is this happening?"

After getting to the airport I called a gay friend of mine for advice. He gave me a phone number for the Servicemembers Legal Defense Network in DC. Their sole job was protecting gay service members affected by the Don't Ask, Don't Tell policy from discrimination and harassment by the military.

I immediately called and told them that I was 90 percent sure the Navy had figured out I was gay, and that in around four hours I was probably going to be interrogated about it. The receptionist immediately transferred me to one of the two lawyers working there at the time. The lawyer was a woman, who managed to calm me down a little. She told me blow by blow what was probably going to happen. I also called Rick and told him to call the lawyers. Rick had no idea what was happening.

After landing in Norfolk, the command master chief picked me up and drove me to the building where Rick worked. He walked me into a conference room, sat me down, and then left. Moments later, a stern female Captain Judge Advocate General walked in and dropped a file in front of me.

She instructed me in a condescending tone, "Open it and read it, Petty Officer Jones."

I opened the folder to find several military documents. It was initially confusing. My eyes scanned over the pages until I found the reason for the investigation. It said that I was suspected of being a "homosexual", and "committing homosexual behavior."

As instructed, I signed the document acknowledging that I'd read it. Then the barrage of questions began. For two hours she tried any way she could to get me to admit that I was gay and in a relationship with Rick. When asked, I simply responded, "I don't feel comfortable with that question. I need to discuss that with my legal counsel."

This infuriated her. She'd orchestrated this meeting without allowing me time to call a lawyer, and was trying to use her advantage to trick me into "telling."

She went on to play the recording that I'd left on Rick's answering machine. Rick had a young female petty officer that worked for him. He'd recently had to counsel her over her poor fitness scores. Apparently she did not like this, and decided to listen to his messages without his knowledge. She found my message and reported it. That was all the Navy needed.

When I was free to go, I walked to the lobby, where the master chief was sitting, and we made our way back to the car. The inside of the car was quiet as he drove me back to my Jeep, which was parked in the SEAL Team parking lot. We must have driven by a broken sewer pipe at some point because most of the five minute drive a faint shitty odor was coming through the vent. After he dropped me off, I thanked him and gave him, what I am sure was, a terrible impression of me smiling in gratitude.

There was a powerful amount of emotion that had been building in-between my sternum and my spine and was pushing upwards with such force that it required every bit of distraction I could muster in my mind. It was so intense that when I went to unlock my Jeep my hands were shaking so badly that it required a deep breath followed by a momentary pause to refocus on the task.

As I drove off the base and headed home, I turned the music up as loud as I could bear. It did not take long after I left the base to realize that I was not going to make it home. I found an empty parking lot in a run-down strip mall. I spotted a secluded area, drove over, and put my vehicle in park. Still shaking, I reached up to the radio and turned it off. I grabbed the steering wheel with both hands and tried to rip it out from the steering column.

"Fuck you! FUCK YOU!" I yelled uncontrollably while still pulling on the steering wheel.

Tears were streaming down my cheeks.

"You can't take this from me!" My breathing had become erratic causing inhales to become involuntary short loud bursts, much like when a child cries.

Feeling frustrated I couldn't pull it off, I let go of the steering wheel and wiped the mucus running from my nose onto the sleeve of my uniform.

Pushing my head against the steering wheel, I clenched my right hand into a fist and held onto it tightly with my left hand. I closed my eyes tensely while the tears ran off the tip of my nose, creating a tiny pool by my feet.

"Please don't take this."

Seconds later, I gave up trying to fight it. I let go of my fist and grabbed the top of the steering wheel above my head, and conceded to the anger, disappointment, and sadness.

An hour later, after pulling into the driveway of the house, I grabbed the rearview mirror and aimed it towards my face. The reflection was far from what I was hoping it would be.

I grabbed my bag from the back of the vehicle and walked into the foyer of the house. I let the bag slide off my shoulder and rest on the floor while I kept walking. Rounding the corner of the room I could see Rick standing behind the counter of the kitchen patiently waiting for me.

As I walked to him, he started moving to meet me halfway. The closer we got to each other; I could tell that he had been crying too. His hands were slowly reaching up to me the closer we got.

We drifted into a tight hug.

"We are going to get through this Rick." I said muffled through the fabric of his shirt.

"Are you ok?" He said softly while turning his head in toward my neck. I squeezed his body and slowly took a step back and placed my hands on his shoulders while he held onto my ribs.

"You wanna get drunk right now?"

"I thought you would never ask." He painfully laughed while wiping his eyes.

CHAPTER 15

Virginia Beach, Va (Part 2)

The following months were humiliating and degrading. All my clearances were pulled. I had to be escorted everywhere I went in my SEAL team building. I even got issued a new ID card with "Escort Required" printed on it in bold red letters. My commanding officer and the command master chief were the only people that knew why I had to be escorted. Surprisingly, they were very kind to me during all of this. They would take extra steps they wouldn't normally do. Simple things like a pat on the back or a, "How ya doing Jones?"

Meanwhile, the rumor mill was going crazy on my team. I could see it in people's faces. That uncomfortably long stare, or quick end to conversations when I came in view became the norm.

The commanding officer pulled me into his office and told me to do whatever I needed to do to take care of this. "Just make a phone call in the morning to check in with us," he said. He did this to allow me to make trips to DC to meet with lawyers and to save me from the embarrassment of walking around the team with an escort like a criminal.

The days I was not in D.C., I repaired small boat engines but mostly washed cars for the support mechanics. The building was located in an area where there were no SEALs or security clearance requirements. It was about two hundred yards away from the SEAL Team Buildings. I often caught myself staring at people coming in and out of the buildings, wishing my life could go back to the way it was before I had been reduced to Navy's highest trained car detailer.

Somehow, my SEAL brothers eventually found out. But they too were surprisingly supportive of me. They would often call me or come by my house to check in on me. It meant a lot to me that they did that. It made me feel bad that I would have ever doubted my brothers to begin with.

The next few months were also very difficult emotionally for me and Rick. Words like "dishonorable discharge" kept getting thrown around. Rick was less than a year from retiring, and could lose all the benefits he had worked so long to earn. On top of my concern for Rick, I was worried about the effect on my name. I had toiled so hard, for so many years, to be the best SEAL that I could be. I had sacrificed so much during my time in the teams; months away from loved ones, brutal climates, hearing loss, deaths of other SEALs, days without sleep, and too many injuries with life long effects to even count... all the things every SEAL sacrifices.

In the midst of the investigation, a gay couple had invited us to come to a party they were having on the beach behind their house. We decided to go. We parked the car, and grabbed a couple beach chairs and towels from the back of the car and made our way around their house to the beach. There was no mistaking where the party was. There were gay flags everywhere surrounding several white pop-up tents providing shade. The music was loud and people were laughing.

After briefly talking to the hosts, we found some available shade in a tent next to a good-looking couple we had never met before. We introduced ourselves, and Rick started setting up our chairs while I went to get us a couple beers.

A few beer trips later, the awkward get-to-know-you small talk ended, and the real conversations began.

Prior to us going, we told ourselves that we were not going to talk about what was going on in our lives. Today we were going to be a normal couple having fun on the beach.

All of us were well into a buzz when they told Rick and I that they were both in the Navy, and had been together for years. One was an officer and the other was a senior enlisted guy.

Rick paused, looked at me, and then told them that we were in the Navy also.

I knew were this was going. It disgusted me because despite the amount of alcohol I drank that day, or the amount I drank since the investigation started, there was just no escaping it. Our days had been littered with hangovers, losing lottery tickets, and pep talks that usually ended with, "One day were going to look back at this and laugh."

Despite my hesitance, having another gay couple in the Navy to talk to was such a tempting refuge for the both of us that I did not even try change the subject.

Over the next 30 minutes, as we talked, I could see their body language start to change. Though they worked hard on being a good ear, I could tell they saw us as a contagious disease instead of what it actually was, just really un-lucky. I could sense their fear of association. A fear the Navy was tracking our moves and would witness us talking to them, or a fear we would rat them out to the Navy in exchange for something.

As painful as the conversation was for them, I know that it made Rick feel better. I on the other hand felt like a pariah.

One day we drove up to DC to meet, on the advice of our lawyers, with a powerful lobbyist. She was an incredibly smart woman and was also a lesbian. As we talked, I could tell things were going in the direction of this becoming a national news story, since that seemed like my only hope for avoiding a dishonorable discharge. She told me to prepare my family for a media circus. She was going to make a couple of calls to try and avoid it, but she warned me to be ready.

I hated the idea, and I loved the idea.

I hated the idea because it seemed like a last-ditch, selfish effort to save my name. Though the world was changing, I knew many people would think lesser of the SEAL community because somehow they would interpret a gay SEAL as a weakness in the selection process, or would negatively feminize the community. I did not want to see the community I loved become a bad gay joke.

I loved the idea because I thought it would be an opportunity to show the world that there are gay people who love this country, and are willing to make God-awful sacrifices for it. It was a chance to argue that we should not be subject to a dishonorable discharge and the consequent inability even to work at McDonald's. I wondered—if there was a chance that it would help the next man or woman, would it be worth it? It was agonizing to think about.

It was only a week later when my commanding officer called me into his office. He sat me down and told me that the case had been dropped.

He went on to tell me that he thought I was a talented SEAL, and hoped that I would stay in the Navy and continue to serve in the teams. My enlistment was about five months from ending, and he knew that. He wanted to put me in a platoon to start training, which would mean finishing my last free-fall jump, but he needed to know that I was going to stay first.

Doing another platoon would be about a two-year commitment. I told him that I needed to think about it. Though I never found out for sure, I had heard that Senator Kerry was the reason why the witch hunt had ended, and why the Navy had been unsuccessful in their efforts to dishonorably discharge me.

The next day, I walked into my commanding officer's office. I blurred my eyes to keep myself distant and told him, "Sir, I don't think I am going to stay. I can't even begin to describe to you what the last three months were like for me. I imagine it is kind of hard for you to understand somebody like me, but I never let my personal life interfere with the mission. Ever. I always wanted to be a SEAL. This place is more than a job; it has been a home for me. I'm not an idiot, I know I got one over on the big Navy, and the powers that be do not like knowing that somewhere in the world is a Navy SEAL like me. I know it will be just be a matter of time before they find another way to kick me out. Only next time, I may not be as lucky."

After getting that out, I actually looked him in the eyes. He smiled at me and asked me how I felt about help instructing a combat swimmer course in Key West before I got out. In my mind, it was his way of letting me know that he felt really bad for what I had gone through. He was a good man.

Rick was able to keep his retirement and leave the Navy on honorable terms. We would end up staying together for many years, but secretly we slowly separated emotionally not long after the Navy. After what had happened, it was as if we had to prove to the world that we could make it as a couple, even if it meant our unhappiness.

I'd rarely taken vacation time while I was in the Navy, and I had almost 120 days saved up. I ended up using all my leave to look for a job before I got out.

I found a job about one month into my search while still technically in the Navy. It was with a small video production company. I had taken acting classes in high school, and also in my spare time in the Navy. It was a great escape, and I learned a lot about people, and myself, in them. The process of taking a story and sharing it with people in a way they can connect with, whether in film or on stage, always fascinated me.

Unfortunately, I ended up hating the job. All I ever did was filing, and the pay was terrible.

In June of 2003, two months into the job, I knew I was going to need more money once the Navy checks stopped coming in. I had a good friend who worked at a shooting range where the SEAL teams often trained. I drove out to talk to him. I told him that if he needed any help on the ranges, even if it meant just cleaning them, to let me know.

He said he actually had something else in mind, and to come back the next day.

When I drove back out to the range, he told me about a job that required guys with my skill set, and that training for it started in a week. He said I would be going to Iraq to protect US dignitaries and interests, and that the pay would be good.

It took a few moments for this to sink in, because for me it was a dream job. I would get to do what I loved most, the thing I was best at, what God put me on this planet to do—protect Americans. The next week we started training, and in that training I got my second name.

My call sign was Bad Monkey.

EPILOGUE

17 Dec 2013

Dear Ethan,

Near-misses happen more than I like to admit, and unfortunately have become a way of life. Today happened to be one of those near-miss days. After taking off all my gear, and thanking my Creator once again, I sluggishly made my way to my room. Pneumonia has been making its rounds (due to the poor air quality and harsh weather), leaving a couple of us miserable in our beds when we are not out doing our thing. Despite my lack of motivation as I write this letter, I can't help but think of the heroic people with whom I have worked.

I have lost some of those brothers, and often like to think about them. I can still hear Hawk's infectious laugh, see Southside's smile, and I think of Scotty every time that '80's hair band music plays.

So many of them have gone, and it's important that I never forget them. Many are fortunately still with us. They all taught me, in their own special ways, how to be more than just a man—something I hope to pass on to you.

Looking out the window, I can see the snow-covered mountains surrounding the war-torn city of Kabul clarified by the light of a glowing full moon. The air is actually kind of clear tonight, which is a welcome relief from the pollution that winter brings to this city. For some reason, the unfriendly weather especially has a way of making me homesick. Perhaps it is because when we are together in my memories, somehow we are always warm.

My initial motivation for writing this book was that I thought it would help bring a little extra income and help the struggling security company that I and your biological father have worked so hard to build. As I started to write more and more, I focused on writing for you, Ethan. In doing so, I was able to be honest with myself.

You now know that your stepdad has travelled down an unconventional road to get to this point in his life. As sometimes unnecessarily difficult as that road might have been, there have always been truths that I could count on.

When you are exhausted, and you feel like you can't go on, sometimes just going through the motions will be enough to get you and others to the finish line. Remember, just showing up is literally half the battle.

Never let somebody's race, religion, sexual orientation, age, or really anything allow you to veil the content of their character. Diversity is one of the greatest gifts this world has to offer. However, diversity without equality in your mind becomes oppression. Once on that road, it becomes harder and harder to change lanes.

Never be afraid to defend yourself or stand by those in righteous need of your defense. The pain of getting beaten up is insignificant compared with what a coward endures every day. Do not associate yourself with cowards; they live for nothing other than themselves. These are incredibly dangerous people. As your biological father always says, quoting Ronald Reagan, "Evil is powerless if the good are unafraid."

Always think about what you say and how it will affect people. A lot of times, not saying anything will make you the smartest man in the room.

Always tell the truth, Ethan, no matter what you think the outcome will be. Most of the time it will not be as bad as you think, but sometimes it will be much worse. People will ultimately respect you for it. With that said, there are extremely rare occasions in life when it is ok. There will be no mistaking the time when it's needed.

If you ever find yourself having to make a tough decision, and not knowing what the right one is, ask yourself which one will be the most difficult for you. Nine times out of ten that is the choice you need to make.

Lastly, and most importantly, I have witnessed how wars, beliefs, miles, and even death seemingly separates families. I know that the love we share as a family, second only to that of our Creator, is the most powerful truth. To comprehend this truth is to understand that distance is an illusion. No matter what the expanse might be, it is ultimately insignificant if our love is unselfish.

No matter what the state of Alabama or anybody else says, we are and always will be a family. Every moment that we are fortunate enough to be together as a family, I know every tragedy, failure, and struggle was worth the pain a million times over. You and your dad make being a father and husband the most remarkable and unexpected accomplishment of my life. There are no words for how thankful I am for you both.

I love you, son,

Brett Jones

CPSIA information can be obtained
at www.ICGtesting.com
Printed in the USA
FFOW04n0629200315
12007FF